HELPING YOUR
DEPRESSED CHILD

How to Order:

Quantity discounts are available from Prima Publishing, P.O. Box 1260BK, Rocklin, CA 95677; telephone (916) 632-4400 . On your letterhead include information concerning the intended use of the books and the number of books you wish to purchase.

HELPING YOUR DEPRESSED CHILD

A Reassuring Guide to the Causes and Treatments of Childhood and Adolescent Depression

Lawrence L. Kerns, M.D.
with Adrienne B. Lieberman

Prima Publishing
P.O. Box 1260BK
Rocklin, CA 95677
(916) 632-4400

Library of Congress Cataloging-in-Publication Data

Kerns, Lawrence.
    Helping your depressed child / Lawrence Kerns with
Adrienne Lieberman.
            p.   cm.
    Includes index.
    ISBN 1-55958-275-8
    1. Depression in children—Popular works.
    I. Lieberman, Adrienne B.   II.   Title.
RJ506.D4K47   1992
618.92′852706—dc20   92-32926
                                                                          CIP

L. L. K.

For my family,
Lawrence A. and Genevieve,
Elizabeth,
Andrew, Caroline, Gillian, and Peter

A. B. L.

For Nancy

CONTENTS

ACKNOWLEDGMENTS

This book grew out of my training and clinical experiences over the past several years. I would like to thank the following teachers and mentors, whose ideas about the treatment of depressed children and their families contributed greatly to my own understanding: Doug Breunlin at the Family Institute of Chicago; Lee Combrinck-Graham, M.D., at the Institute for Juvenile Research; Richard Marohn, M.D., at Northwestern University Medical School; and Paul Tolpin, M.D., at the Chicago Institute for Psychoanalysis. Each has given me the benefits of his or her unique wisdom over a number of years and many discussions.

I also wish to thank the staff of the Good Shepherd Hospital Mental Health Units, the Partial Hospital Programs of Lake County, and Family Services of McHenry County. As a team we have treated hundreds of children, adolescents, and their families. I am sure I learned more from them than they learned from me.

I am eternally grateful to and continually impressed by the experts who have created this book with me, including my co-author, Adrienne B. Lieberman; our literary agent,

Jane Jordan Browne; our editors, Jennifer Basye and Anne
Montague; and our production editor, Janelle Rohr.

Finally, and most importantly, I want to thank the children and their families who provided both the substance of
and the reason for this book. Your words and lives will
provide comfort to many families.

INTRODUCTION

M**ary** doesn't seem to care about her work anymore. She'll say she's excited about something, but there's no enthusiasm in her voice; it's flat. She doesn't seem to like herself much; she doesn't care what happens to her."

Does Mary sound like someone you know—perhaps a co-worker, a relative, or friend? This description could fit any number of depressed adults, but Mary is an 8-year-old girl. Sadly, she has lots of company.

As many as 6 million children and adolescents in the United States—about 10 percent of our children—are depressed. Not just a little blue, or sad once in a while, or bored, or lonely, or worried, but suffering from a serious and potentially fatal illness: depression.

Depression makes life miserable for children. It gets in the way of their normal development, sapping the energy they need to work in school and play at home. Depressed children desperately need help, but a child's depression may drive loved ones away precisely when the child needs them most. Unnoticed, depression can lead to suicide, even in children as young as 5.

For many years the medical profession denied that depression existed in children. Two mistaken beliefs led doctors to this conclusion.

For one thing, many psychiatrists believed that children's "carefree" lives didn't contain enough stress to cause depression. They were wrong. In fact, children can and do wrestle with a variety of serious problems. Divorce, a death in the family, even a move—any of these stresses can plunge a vulnerable child into depression.

Psychiatrists also used to assume that depression resulted from an overly critical conscience, or superego. Because the superego doesn't develop fully until late childhood, doctors concluded that young children could not become depressed. But today we understand that depression has many possible causes. Most psychiatrists no longer believe that a malfunctioning superego is the sole origin of depression.

The very idea of childhood depression makes adults feel nervous, perhaps even a little depressed ourselves. We want to be able to kiss every hurt and make it better. Failing that, we'd just as soon escape. If we can put childhood depression out of our minds, we won't have to face our own helplessness. But ignoring childhood depression will not make it go away.

Indeed, the American Medical Association recently reported the grim fact that mental disorders have become the leading disability among 10- to 18-year-olds in this country, far outnumbering all other chronic physical and medical conditions. A national survey of eighth- and tenth- grade students yielded the following statistics:

- 61 percent of the students reported feeling depressed and hopeless.
- 45 percent claimed they had trouble coping with stressful situations at home and school.
- 36 percent felt they often or sometimes had nothing to look forward to.
- 34 percent had considered committing suicide, and 14 percent had actually attempted it. Indeed, for every completed suicide, between 50 and 200 attempts are probably made. Many of these go unnoticed or unreported.

Despite these sobering findings, experts estimate that less than 20 percent of children with serious emotional problems receive any treatment at all. Deluged with cases, many child mental health agencies have such long waiting lists that a child can't even be seen for an evaluation for weeks. School social workers encounter so many depressed children that they must budget their time scrupulously just to address the most severe cases. I have sometimes been consulted about five suicidal adolescents in a single week.

The good news is that childhood depression *can* be treated. You *can* get help and you *can* help your child get better.

The first step is to determine whether your child is depressed. Surprisingly, your child may be deeply depressed even if he doesn't look sad or doesn't say he's unhappy. Childhood depression frequently masquerades as temper tantrums, truancy, drug abuse, or eating disorders.

In this book, you'll learn about the many masks childhood depression can wear. You'll also discover why children get depressed and the important role you play in helping your child deal constructively with these feelings.

Depressed people—children or adults—frequently feel a loss of control, a sense of helplessness. Therapy may be necessary for your child to regain a sense of being in charge of his own life. In this book, we'll outline how to select a competent therapist for your depressed child and how to evaluate several different types of therapy, including medication. You'll also find information on hospitalization, should your child need that kind of intensive help.

But the most important source of help your depressed child has is you, her parents. That's because not only do you love your child more than anyone else in the world, you also know your own child best. The things you do and say have a profound impact on her. At best, a good therapist merely stands in as an agent for you. You and your spouse actually share a golden opportunity to be "therapeutic" for your child for years to come.

The way you choose to think about your child, your family, and depression determines what you will choose to do about it and how successful you will be. Rather than viewing you and your child as defective, I look at your child and your family as fundamentally competent. On the assumption that you already have the skills you need to help your own child, I will try to show you how to put your own skills to work. This book will also teach you about "systems" such as the family, the school, and the neighborhood. You'll learn to look for ways your child's depression may reflect solvable problems in these various systems.

My approach takes into account the normal developmental processes that occur within your child and your family. Growth, after all, is your child's developmental task, and she has a self-righting tendency on her side. Because she's still growing, she can more easily bob up and resume course, like a capsized sailboat. My major goal is to help you and your depressed child clear away the obstacles that are temporarily blocking her from normal growth.

HOW TO READ THIS BOOK

Of course, we hope you'll eventually read the entire book. But you certainly don't have to read it in order, and it may be best for you to go directly to the chapter that addresses your particular concerns.

For example, you may have picked up this book because you're wondering whether your child is depressed. If you can't tell, you're not alone. You may want to look first at Chapter 2, which describes the many ways depression can announce itself in children and adolescents. Chapters 4 through 6 examine some common manifestations of childhood depression in much greater detail.

If your child has been diagnosed with depression, your biggest question may be "Why?" Chapter 3 explores that important question. Or you may be wondering how your family will cope (Chapter 8) or how to select a psychotherapist (Chapter 9).

Perhaps your child has attempted suicide or has given you reason to fear he might. Chapter 7 would probably be a good place for you to begin. If you've been told that your depressed child might need to be hospitalized, read Chapters 10 and 11, which will help you evaluate that advice and come to the best decision.

If you need more specialized information, the "For Further Reading" list should help you find it. In addition, many of the organizations cited in the Resources section offer support and further information for the price of a stamp or a phone call.

Your child's depression may be the most frightening thing that ever happened to your family. But childhood depression can also provide an opportunity for real growth, for all of you.

I

WHAT IS CHILDHOOD DEPRESSION?

___

1

CHILDHOOD DEPRESSION: A CLOSER LOOK

Seriously depressed children frequently fall behind in school and some never catch up. They may lose friends and undo accomplishments they can never regain. Sometimes depressed children engage in destructive or self-destructive behavior. And behind the 6 million depressed children and adolescents stand their families, who suffer tremendously as well.

THE EFFECTS OF CHILDHOOD DEPRESSION

School Failure and Family Frustration

Kathy, a depressed 10-year-old, also has marked learning difficulties. Kathy's parents described the daily ordeal of helping their daughter with her homework. Every night after dinner they all sit at the dining room table. Kathy

3

works for a while, but as soon as she encounters a difficult problem she begins to squirm.

As her parents struggle to keep her focused on the task, Kathy grows increasingly uncooperative. If she doesn't end up running from the table in tears, she provokes her parents until they send her away with a punishment.

Kathy and her family face a daily trial, a confrontation with their greatest fears. Every day the girl goes to school expecting to fail and to feel miserable in the process. Then each night after dinner, as their daughter flounders over the simplest math problem, her parents face their own shame and failure.

Convinced their child is defective, Kathy's parents must also face their own inadequacy. In their frustration, they argue with Kathy and each other until they finally fall asleep in exhaustion. Naturally, they all dread the repetition of this cycle the next day.

Behavior Problems

Your depressed child may engage in a variety of self-destructive behaviors, such as lying, stealing, fighting, ditching classes, or even running away from home, to avoid facing his feelings. Indeed, a child's depression frequently goes unnoticed because his misbehavior is so distracting and annoying. Sometimes it's simply less painful for a child to act up than to feel down. But the possible results of a depressed child's actions, including a criminal record, may imperil his future.

Drug Abuse

Depression can easily lead to drug use in a desperate attempt to "self-medicate" the pain an adolescent simply can't understand. As one depressed 16-year-old put it,

"When I first tried drugs, I didn't get high, I just came up to ground level. But it was certainly better than where I'd been and I knew it. Even now when I use drugs, I don't feel high—I just feel better. When I'm not taking drugs, I feel like shit."

A Threat to Your Child's Future

Depression can interfere with a child's development, canceling achievements that may have taken years to build. Tara, 17, got depressed in September of her senior year. This high-powered student excelled in both academics and gymnastics. Everyone expected her to win the state championship and to be awarded a scholarship to Yale. But all these expectations overwhelmed her.

"The worst thing for me is that I'm disappointing them," Tara said. "My dad, my mom, my coach . . . they've done everything for me and I'm letting them down. But I can't say that to them. My dad thinks that asking for help is a sign of weakness, and he only admires strength. If I tell them I'm scared I won't win state this year, or that there's too much pressure, they'll think I'm too sensitive or too weak."

Even her depression was a burden Tara felt she had to shoulder alone. "I don't like it when they worry about me. I don't like it when they get upset because I'm depressed. It's my problem and I want to handle it myself. But they want me to be ecstatic about myself, delighted about what a great future I have. Can't they see that their expectation that I be happy all the time is hard on me, too?"

When the pressure inside her got too great, Tara felt she needed to hurt herself to feel better. So she would burn herself with a curling iron or cut herself with a razor. When she saw the blood or blisters and felt pain, Tara's tension flowed out as if she had opened a drain. But soon even these actions weren't enough. Tara flunked two courses that semester, and failed to qualify for the state gymnastics competition.

Depression in childhood puts a child at increased risk for further episodes of depression both during childhood and through adulthood. At least half the children who experience a clinical depression will go on to have subsequent bouts of the illness.

That's why it's vitally important to diagnose depression early and to treat it adequately. The medical profession has come a long way since the days when psychiatrists denied the very existence of childhood depression. But many parents continue to do so.

FACING UP TO YOUR CHILD'S DEPRESSION

To see a child suffering hurts any adult, but for a parent it is excruciating. When your child's depression fails to lift, you feel more and more distressed yourself.

Your child's inconsolable sadness may make you try to ignore it in the hope that it will go away. You tell yourself, "It's just a phase. She'll get over it."

I recently treated a 14-year-old girl whose depression made her whole family extremely uncomfortable. In our family therapy sessions, as soon as Diane began to talk about her sadness one of two things would always happen. Either her father would turn to me and ask a theoretical question about himself, or her younger brother would start to misbehave.

Both behaviors served temporarily to distract Diane and her entire family from Diane's depression. But her sadness didn't go away, and in fact she began to get worse.

When I eventually interrupted her father's and brother's attempts to distract her, Diane finally expressed her feelings in tears and her mother joined her. As her mother held her, cried with her, and comforted her, Diane's father wept openly for the first time in 12 years. Only after they were finally able to acknowledge Diane's depression could her family begin to work together to do something about it. Your family, too, may have to abandon the long-standing strategies you have used to deny that your child is depressed.

Taking Prompt Action

The sooner you can recognize your child's depression, the easier it will be to treat. Once depressive behaviors become habits, they become harder to abandon. Recognizing and treating depression early minimizes the consequences that can prove so difficult to reverse: school failure, injured self-image, pain and suffering, disrupted and lost friendships, and family conflict.

You also need to move quickly because depression interferes with your child's normal development. A depressed child has trouble taking initiative, becoming independent, developing competence, and establishing an identity. Until he finds relief for his depression, your child will not be able to get on with the business of growing up.

Robert's school called me because the 9-year-old boy had threatened to kill himself by dunking a radio in his bathtub. A bright child with inquisitive blue eyes, Robert boasted an exceptional memory and could recall things that happened when he was 2 years old. Unfortunately, he retained a vivid memory of his mother's death from a drug overdose when he was 5.

After being bounced between several relatives, Robert had ended up with his aunt. Now it was time to decide whether this temporary arrangement should be made permanent.

Recently, Robert had stopped doing his work in school and had quit playing with other children. The boy had also lost his appetite, gaining no weight in months. The small items Robert stole from neighborhood stores were things his aunt would have bought him if only he had asked. But the sad child never asked and his aunt hesitated to scold him for his stealing.

Abandonment often figures prominently in childhood depression. When a child's needs go unmet, he may experience physical or psychological abandonment. Robert experienced both kinds of desertion. First his mother took her own life, and then the boy suffered psychological abandonment when he was passed from relative to relative.

Finally, Robert's aunt took him in, but she was tormented by her own fears of being deserted by the people she loved. In her insecurity, she wondered whether she could possibly make a good parent. Therapy helped Robert's aunt recognize how important she was to her nephew. She also learned to appreciate her strengths: her good humor, her commitment, and her professional talents.

In therapy with Robert and other depressed children, I always try to find workable solutions to specific problems. Robert, for example, had complained that he didn't know how to make friends. So I gave him the assignment to study the kids at school, in order to figure out how they acted with each other and made friends. The next week Robert gave me a detailed analysis of the importance of the popular video game Nintendo in the social life of 9-year-old boys. Then he took it on himself to practice and read about Nintendo, and start talking with the other kids at school. Robert was pleasantly surprised to learn that they listened to him.

Meanwhile, Robert's aunt learned how to determine when her nephew needed comforting for his sadness and when he required appropriate discipline. For example, she stopped accepting Robert's repeated claim that no one in his class would come if he invited a child over to play. One week, Robert's aunt simply told him to ask a boy over by Friday or she would do it for him. To save himself the embarrassment, Robert invited someone, and the boy soon became his friend.

Today, Robert is succeeding in school. He enjoys friendships with three or four boys and was finally adopted by his aunt. Robert's depression vanished three months after his first visit.

DEPRESSION IN ADOLESCENCE

New issues surface as youngsters reach adolescence. During the teen years, children need to do more than merely get along at home, at school, and at play. They must now begin to separate from their parents.

The adolescent must learn to accept complete responsibility for his thoughts, feelings, and behavior. He needs to begin to make important decisions for himself without being bound by what his parents would do or say in the same situation. Depression in adolescence frequently stems from a child's ambivalence about achieving this crucial step.

Growing up doesn't happen overnight, of course. Children gradually move away from physical, then psychological, dependence on their parents. A healthy adolescent can eventually leave home and pursue her life without constant worry about what her parents might think of her decisions. She can form intimate relationships without needing to replace a parent or make up for something she missed as a child. Healthy adolescents can separate from their parents without having to reject them completely or deny the important contributions they have made.

Faced with this daunting task, it's no wonder many adolescents get anxious, angry, or depressed. Anxious adolescents seem unable to make any decisions. They become more dependent on their parents, seeking to cling to them instead of moving ahead on their own. Angry adolescents engage in rebellious behavior. Spurning everything their parents value, they show how much space they need to put between themselves and their parents. Some teens, like Brad, become depressed.

Brad came into the hospital at 17 with depression and suicidal thoughts, along with a lengthy history of running away from home and skipping school. Brad strode onto the psychiatric unit dressed entirely in black, with a shock of freshly dyed magenta hair and a silver earring. He had gotten caught in the dilemma that frequently faces adolescent children: If they don't leave home angry, they may not be able to leave home at all.

Brad's parents were conservative, middle-class people who believed in working hard and keeping a low profile. They were shocked by Brad's defiant and sometimes dramatic behavior, and they alternated between getting angry at him for being a selfish ingrate and blaming themselves for provoking his rebellion. Although adolescents must struggle to separate from their parents, they frequently lack the necessary coping skills to do so. Brad, for example, couldn't look realistically at his own strengths and weaknesses. As many adolescents do, he fluctuated between a grandiose sense of his abilities and a harsh denial that he had any value whatsoever.

After two weeks in the hospital, Brad began to develop a more positive sense of his identity as a sensitive young man and a potentially successful student. In therapy, I acknowledged and encouraged Brad's strengths, like his artistic talent. As a result, Brad learned to accept his own talent and be proud of it.

A therapist may have better luck than parents with this task. An adolescent struggles against mutually irreconcilable wishes. On one hand, he longs to have his parents rescue, protect, and unequivocally admire him. But at the same time, the internal war he wages against these infantile strivings may force him to reject all parental support.

In working with Brad and his parents, I helped the boy negotiate an agreement that allowed him a fair amount of freedom at home. But the contract also spelled out Brad's willingness to follow a reasonable set of family rules.

MAINTAINING PERSPECTIVE

As serious as childhood depression is and as urgently as your child may need treatment, you have everything to be hopeful about. Depression can be treated, your child can get better, and his life can be saved. In fact, when researchers examined the childhoods of 400 of the most eminent persons in the 20th century, they found that 60 percent of these tremendously successful people—people like Thomas Edison and Pablo Picasso—had suffered serious problems during childhood.

One such child appeared "shy, lonely, and withdrawn from the world." His teachers considered him mentally slow and unsociable. The boy's halting speech made his parents think he was dull. Unable to tolerate school, this child tried to stay away by getting his doctor to say he'd had a nervous breakdown. Later he failed his college entrance examinations and had to go back to high school. Then Albert Einstein went on to change the course of history.

Of course, each child has unique problems and strengths, so individual families will have to seek unique solutions. If you think your child is depressed, you'll need plenty of information and encouragement. You'll find both here. Armed with this book, and fully aware of your choices, you can now begin to help your child *help himself* to get better.

2

Is Your Child Depressed?

——

You may be wondering how you can tell whether your child is depressed. Indeed, it can be hard to pinpoint. Childhood depression frequently hides behind more easily identifiable problems such as school failure and social withdrawal. Even the most sensitive parent may not recognize the signs.

Mrs. Jenks, for example, brought her daughter Felice, 8, to see me because the third-grader couldn't get her work done in class and kept forgetting to turn in her homework. "It's just not like her," Mrs. Jenks said, bewildered. "She's always been such a good student."

Felice's teacher agreed that the girl seemed bright enough, but described her as "preoccupied." Reflecting on Felice's behavior in school, her teacher noted: "You know, Felice hasn't made any real friends. She's very quiet and keeps to herself at recess. Usually, she spends her time wandering around the playground alone or sitting by herself on a bench."

Felice was new at this school. When her father lost his job, the whole family suddenly had to leave the town that had been their home for 15 years.

Even so, her mother assumed Felice was handling the move well. She described her daughter as "a precocious child, mature for her age. Before we moved, I talked with Felice about setting a good example for her younger brother and sister. In fact, I thought Felice took the move better than anyone else in the family."

Mrs. Jenks assured me that Felice was a cheerful child who always tried to lift everyone else's spirits. "I haven't noticed Felice crying around the house," she said, surprised when I asked whether her daughter seemed sad.

Felice, too, maintained that things were just fine. But the look in the little girl's eyes belied her words. When I asked if she missed her old friends, Felice's eyes filled up and overflowed. She sobbed, "Rebecca was my best friend. She lived right next door and we were always in the same class. We were on a soccer team and Brownies together, too. We did everything together."

Discussing the loss of her friend unleashed a flood of tears. Felice sobbed, "I didn't even know we were moving until a week before we left. My dad got this job and we had to go right away. I hardly had a chance to say goodbye to Rebecca."

Once Felice realized that she didn't have to protect me from her sadness, she revealed for the first time how awful she felt. Indeed, this child had neither a learning problem nor a socialization problem. Felice was depressed.

Preoccupied with her own feelings of loss, Mrs. Jenks had failed to notice how sad her daughter was. Indeed, parents frequently have a difficult time detecting depression in their children.

In this chapter, you'll learn some ways of talking and listening to your child that may make her more likely to share her real feelings with you. You'll also discover how to differentiate clinical depression from normal sad feelings.

Finally, we will consider bipolar disorder, commonly known as manic-depression.

You needn't shoulder the entire responsibility for diagnosing your child's depression; you'll want to enlist professional help for that. But knowing some of the signs of depression can certainly alert you to the need for such help. What's more, you'll become an active participant in the diagnostic process.

WHY YOU MAY NOT NOTICE DEPRESSION

Like Mrs. Jenks, you may never have dreamed that your child was depressed. Many children won't say they're feeling sad unless you ask them. And, like Felice, some children won't even acknowledge it then. Some of the symptoms of depression—low self-esteem, pessimism about the future, and persistent fatigue—can be well masked by a depressed child.

So if you're having trouble identifying your child's depression, you're not alone. In 1988, researchers from the Houston Child Guidance Center found that parents seldom knew about a variety of symptoms their depressed children had reported to the researchers. These symptoms included negative feelings, decreased energy, difficulty concentrating, and sleep disturbances. Not surprisingly, parents noticed overt symptoms such as excessive crying or complaining, but remained largely unaware of the more subtle signs.

Have you talked to your spouse about your child's symptoms? In the Houston study, fathers and mothers agreed on the presence of symptoms more often than did parents and their children. When one parent knew of a child's suicidal thoughts, in 88 percent of the cases the other parent shared the knowledge. But only about one parent in three was even aware of a child's suicidal thoughts.

If you are depressed yourself, you may not have the energy to recognize the signs of depression in your child. Sad about her family's unexpected move, Mrs. Jenks failed to notice how depressed her daughter was.

On the other hand, your own depression may make you even more sensitive to your children's sadness. Several research studies concur that depressed parents seem to spot symptoms of childhood depression more accurately than parents who are not depressed. Indeed, a depressed parent may be all too aware of the many ways depression distorts thinking, creates unpleasant feelings, and even produces physical discomfort.

You may also be more apt to notice the symptoms of depression in your child if he is moderately depressed than if he is severely depressed. The Houston researchers found that children reported *fewer* symptoms once they crossed the threshold from moderately to severely depressed. I've often noticed in my own practice that a moderately depressed child may be quite open about how he feels when asked, while a more severely depressed child may deny symptoms or say "I don't know," as if it's hardly worth the effort to talk about it.

If your child is an adolescent, her age-appropriate uncommunicativeness may make depression even harder to discern. But regardless of your child's age, the first thing you need to do is talk and listen to her.

TALKING AND LISTENING TO YOUR CHILD

Getting children to talk about their feelings can be tricky. Some children say very little much of the time and most children say very little at least some of the time. A younger child may not yet know how to put his feelings into words. Older children may not want to put their feelings into words, especially "bad" or sad feelings. Even many adults have a hard time talking about depression. Talking can make some depressed people feel worse, especially if the listener doesn't understand or doesn't seem to care.

But statements such as "I don't feel like going to school today," "Nobody plays with me on the playground," "I'm dumb," or "I miss Sportie" should prompt you to invite further discussion. Be attentive, patient, and accepting so your child can say whatever she wants to about the subject.

It may be quite painful for you to hear her express sad feelings, but try to restrain your impulse to jump in right away. Even if you long to make your child feel better, she really needs you to listen and try to understand.

Avoid saying things that deny the validity of your child's feelings. Statements such as "You don't really mean that," "You don't really feel that way," "You shouldn't be sad; you've got so much going for you," or "Don't feel bad; we'll get you a new dog" will cut off the conversation with your child before it even begins.

Simply let your child speak without correcting, criticizing, or trying to fix whatever is wrong. Accept your child's feelings even though they may be painful to hear. If your child doesn't volunteer how he feels, you can try probing gently to get him to talk. But to do this, you need to know what's going on in your child's life.

Let's say your daughter is eager to play on her school's basketball team. You need to recognize how important this is to her, how nervous she is, and how she'll feel if she doesn't make the team. Make sure you know when the tryouts will be. Don't bug her about it or get more involved than she wants you to be, but let her know you're aware of how hard she's practicing and how much she wants to make it. Offer help and give her plenty of moral support. Acknowledge her nervousness. Be aware of when she'll hear about the results, and be prepared to acknowledge her feelings, good or bad. Consider in advance how you'll help her deal with her success or failure.

But most important, remember to let her have her own feelings. Allow her to express them without your correction or attempt to make her feel differently.

If your child doesn't bring up depressed feelings on her own, you might make an observation: "You seem kind of down since you got that report card," or "I haven't heard you talk about Colleen lately and you seem a little lonely." Such statements demonstrate that you notice what's going on, you're alert to nonverbal signals about how your child is feeling, and you're eager to listen.

If an open-ended observation doesn't produce a conversation, you might try following up with a gentle question: "I haven't heard you talk about Colleen lately . . . is everything okay?" or "I know you were disappointed by your grades . . . is that still bothering you?" Such statements require a judgment on your part about what's troubling your child. But even if you miss the mark, your child may still volunteer what is really wrong.

You might also try sharing your own feelings. "I really miss Grandpa . . . sometimes I think about him and just start crying," or "It's hard for me not to know whether Daddy will get this transfer and whether we'll have to move . . . it must be hard for you, too."

Don't get so carried away with your feelings that you miss the goal of enabling your child to talk about his sad feelings. Children should know that their parents feel strongly about things, but it's not your child's responsibility to comfort you.

WHAT'S NORMAL SADNESS AND WHAT'S DEPRESSION?

How will you know whether your child's sad feelings constitute depression or are normal? If you're confused about exactly what "normal" is, don't be alarmed. Even the "experts" have a hard time defining normal.

When we ask the question "What is normal?" we have to define which "normal" we mean: average, free of disease, or optimally healthy. We must also specify: normal for whom? at what age? under what circumstances?

A "normal" reaction to a move to a new city and a new school will differ radically from a "normal" reaction to starting the new school year in one's old school in the same neighborhood with the same friends.

It certainly was normal for Felice Jenks to be sad about moving away from her old friends, school, and neighborhood. It was also normal for Felice to feel bad about her father's disappointing job loss, especially since it preoccupied the rest of the family. But life stresses like these shouldn't make a child feel hopeless. She shouldn't get so depressed that she can't concentrate in school or make some new friends.

Mrs. Jenks finally noticed Felice's depression when it led to school failure. Gentle probing about how Felice felt about leaving her best friend might have revealed it even earlier.

Normal Feelings

Before we discuss the symptoms of depression, let's take a brief look at "normal" feelings. What kinds of feelings do children of a given age usually experience, and when is it normal for your child to feel sad?

INFANCY We're all born with an innate capacity to feel emotions. Babies demonstrate at least seven distinct emotions in the first months of life: joy, anger, surprise, disgust, interest, and sadness. So the capacity for sadness exists in every newborn.

In fact, depression can strike even in infancy. In the 1940s, Dr. Rene Spitz, a pioneer in infant mental health,

observed what he termed "anaclitic depression" in infants
who had suffered an early separation from their mothers.
Deprived of adequate emotional stimulation, these babies
fed poorly and didn't gain weight. They appeared listless
and unhappy, failing to smile or respond to attempts at
engaging them. Eventually, most of the babies did respond
to sensitive caregiving.

At around 1 year of age, most of your baby's feelings
revolved around a sense of trust in you. She probably began
to express some normal anxiety about moving away from
you as she ventured further out into the world.

TODDLERHOOD   Between 1 and 3, your toddler wrestled
with issues of autonomy and control. Your efforts to limit
her may have provoked intense anger. Her principal negative emotion, shame, was probably covered up by frequent
temper displays.

The normal toddler develops rudimentary social skills by
learning to channel the aggressiveness she feels when her
wishes are thwarted. Periodic sadness about separation
from parents is normal for this age. So are periodic defiant
reactions to frustration.

THE PRESCHOOL YEARS   From 3½ to 6, a child's dependence on her mother lessens as she discovers other interesting people. This time may be characterized by rapid shifts
in allegiance between mother and father, and equally
rapid shifts between love and anger. Brash self-confidence
or even aggressiveness may alternate with regressions to
more childish behavior. Preschool children become progressively more capable of thinking before acting, of playing cooperatively with peers, of making friendships, and of
getting along with parents and siblings. The normal preschool child develops increasing initiative without feeling
guilty over harming others with her success.

SCHOOL AGE   The normal school-age child appears proud
and self-confident. A child's industriousness drives her to

work toward competence in academics, social skills, and physical accomplishments. As she moves away from complete dependence on her parents, she begins to rely more on friends and teachers for support. The healthy child enjoys new experiences, makes friends easily, shows competitive feelings without being aggressive, and acts freely without being impulsive. She follows rules and respects others' rights. From time to time, she gets sad, but she can use her family and friends to buoy herself.

Of course, as your child begins to enter the world at large she becomes increasingly vulnerable to failure and disappointment. For some children, the school years prove to be a time of learning difficulties as well as social ostracism. School-age children may react to such troubles with depression rather than with the misbehavior that characterizes a younger child.

ADOLESCENCE   Adolescence is the stage of psychological adaptation to the biological events of puberty, dramatic hormonal shifts and physical maturation. Children seem to take one of three routes through this stage of life, according to the research findings of Dr. Harvey Golombek of the University of Toronto.

About 35 percent of adolescents follow a "stable clear route." These children maintain confidence that they can handle life's challenges. They hold positive attitudes, seem generally happy, and maintain affectionate relationships with both family and peers. They're rarely anxious, depressed, or hateful, and they never report serious turmoil. As one mother put it, " I kept expecting Jill to be a 'terrible teenager,' but she never went through that stage."

Another 40 percent of adolescents appear to follow a "fluctuating route." These teens demonstrate alternating periods of anxious or depressed feelings, related to a specific stress. Emotionally stable at times, they seem quite distressed at other times. They vary in expressing optimistic and affectionate feelings, and their self-esteem fluctuates wildly. One father complained, "I can never really tell from one day to the next how Joel's going to feel and act. He's just like springtime in Chicago." The "fluctuating" group experiences considerably more anxiety, depression, and anger than the "stable clear" group. Their parents probably do, too.

The remaining 25 percent of adolescents seem to follow a "stable disturbed route." Disturbed teens experience obvious and persistent problems in personality functioning throughout adolescence. Others view them as untrustworthy, and they demonstrate lingering confusion about their own identities. This group experiences difficulty adjusting to academic and social demands. Many of them are chronically anxious and depressed. Not surprisingly, a good percentage of adolescents from this group come to psychiatric attention.

Adolescence itself has several stages. For some children, the onset of puberty—a cataclysmic physical, hormonal, and emotional change—often ushers in a limited period of disequilibrium. A new adolescent normally questions previously accepted values, ideals, and beliefs, and understandably feels "mixed up" at times. But while temporary periods of depressed mood are normal, an adolescent shouldn't suffer the disturbances of sleep, appetite, and thinking that mark a major depression.

After passing through puberty, young people tend to appear happier and more relaxed. But the middle adolescent's new self-image remains fragile and needs frequent reassurance from the all-important peer group. "Sharon's on the phone constantly," complained one frustrated mother. "It's as though she's grown a new umbilical cord." By turns, your middle adolescent may feel arrogant and superior, then weak and inferior.

Your teen's biggest challenge is to declare psychological independence from you. When a parent says or does something that stimulates unspoken fears of dependence, a typical adolescent may erupt into verbal defiance. As one mother put it, "Jack's like a kettle on the fire, always about to boil over."

Your older adolescent will focus on defining her identity and on creating intimate relationships. Once the challenges of adulthood begin to loom large, a young adult without a secure sense of self may be swamped by the anxiety and depression that can characterize any difficult transition.

CHARACTERISTICS OF CLINICAL DEPRESSION

You can see that periods of depressed mood make up a normal part of your child's or your adolescent's life. You can even expect such periods at times of stress or change, especially following such serious losses as the death of a loved one or the loss of a good friend.

So how can you tell whether your child needs treatment for a clinical depression? Three characteristics distinguish normal depressed moods from a depressive disorder: how much (degree), how deep (pervasiveness), and how long (duration). A major depressive disorder isn't a passing sad mood, but involves a marked disturbance of mood that persists for most of the day, nearly every day, and lasts for at least two weeks.

Although depression may be accompanied by biological changes, it can't be determined solely by a blood test or another laboratory test. A therapist must diagnose depression by observing and interviewing your child and by talking to you and other people who are familiar with your child's symptoms, his mood, and his behavior. Becoming aware of the signs of depression can alert you to seek the professional help your child may need.

Therapists diagnose depression according to the criteria cited in the *Diagnostic and Statistical Manual of Mental Disorders, Third Revised Edition (DSM-III-R)*. The box on page 25 lists criteria, at least five of which must persist for two weeks or more to qualify for a diagnosis of clinical depression.

Dysthymia

This form of depression is less severe but longer lasting than major depression. To be diagnosed with dysthymia, children and adolescents must show depressed mood or irritability lasting at least one year. The symptoms listed in the box—appetite disturbance, sleep disruption, fatigue, and low self-esteem—chronically plague the dysthymic child, but in a milder form.

NOTICING DEPRESSION IN YOUR CHILD

Depressed Mood

If your child is depressed, she will typically show a low or deflated mood, though some children or adolescents may be persistently irritable. Indeed, a depressed mood is the *sine qua non* of major depression.

Depressed children frequently describe themselves as bored, but the boredom of depression has no connection to what they are doing. This boredom never goes away.

Other depressed children say they feel lonely. Rachel, 14, put it this way: "Sometimes at school, in the hall during class change with the noise and the crowds all around me, I still feel alone and sort of lost."

DIAGNOSTIC CRITERIA FOR A
MAJOR DEPRESSIVE EPISODE

- Depressed mood (can be irritable mood in children and adolescents) most of the day, nearly every day, as indicated either by subjective account or observation by others
- Markedly diminished interest or pleasure in all, or almost all, activities most of the day, nearly every day (as indicated either by subjective account or observation by others of apathy most of the time)
- Significant weight loss or weight gain when not dieting (more than 5 percent of body weight in a month), or decrease or increase in appetite nearly every day (in children, consider failure to gain expected weight)
- Insomnia or hypersomnia nearly every day
- Fatigue or loss of energy nearly every day
- Psychomotor agitation or retardation nearly every day (observable by others, not merely subjective feelings of restlessness or being slowed down)
- Feelings of worthlessness or excessive or inappropriate guilt (which may be delusional) nearly every day (not merely self-reproach or guilt about being sick)
- Diminished ability to think or concentrate, or indecisiveness, nearly every day (either by subjective account or as observed by others)
- Recurrent thoughts of death (not just fear of dying), recurrent suicidal ideation without a specific plan, or a suicide attempt or a specific plan for committing suicide

In my clinical work with children, especially preadolescents, I often witness a sense of loneliness coinciding with a child's active attempts to isolate herself from others. Your depressed child may be unable to stand the stimulation of being with others, but being alone may make her anxious. The noted British psychoanalyst D. W. Winnicott concluded that a child's ability to tolerate aloneness derived from being comfortably "alone" with her mother. To Winnicott, this kind of being alone meant being quietly occupied with one's own thoughts while being simultaneously fully aware of a parent's reassuring presence. According to Winnicott, a child who has experienced this safe kind of aloneness gradually internalizes a sense of comfort with being alone.

But some depressed children seem to have lost the capacity to be alone. Instead, they may get restless when no one else is around, even though they're equally miserable in the company of others. In free play during recess at school, depressed children seem to spend more time isolated or engaged in fights than children who are not depressed.

If your child is depressed, he may cry over things that ordinarily would not have upset him. One mother reported, "When I told Mike to remake his bed, he burst into angry tears." Your child may seem more easily bothered by things or simply appear more fragile and unhappy.

Your depressed child may also stop smiling. One of the earliest infant social behaviors, smiling is a powerful instrument of bonding. Throughout life, smiling continues to advertise a person's happiness. The disappearance of smiling is a neon sign announcing that a problem exists.

But depressed children haven't merely lost the ability to smile. These children simply can't be cheered up no matter how hard their friends or family try. Joey, 10, had been depressed for several months. His 13-year-old sister told me, "I used to be able to make him laugh. We always did silly things to get each other going. But nothing makes him laugh anymore. . . . Even I can't cheer him up."

Some children experience depression not so much as sadness but as emptiness. This emptiness suggests a loss of the inner drive that can make a person of any age feel fulfilled. Tony, 11, described it this way: "I feel like my insides are empty."

Tony expressed himself well and was used to putting his feelings into words. But many children that age won't say what they're feeling, especially if no one asks. They may just say "I feel fine," as Felice did. If you probe further or wait for a time when your child seems to want to talk, you may get a clearer explanation. But many times you will simply have to infer how your child is feeling.

A sensory blunting that goes along with depression can make your depressed child feel numb and appear impassive. Debbie, 13, practically whispered, "I'm unhappy all the time, but I don't think I show it. It's not that I try to cover it up, I just don't show anything . . . I can't. I don't think anybody knows how unhappy I am."

Anger

One theory of depression explains it as anger directed inward against the self, but anger may erupt at others as well. Your depressed child may seem particularly irritable, a young child throwing temper tantrums and an older child becoming argumentative. Your child's anger may overflow simply because he feels so sad inside.

Loss of Interest or Pleasure

Whether or not your child acknowledges a disturbance of mood, note if she loses interest in activities she used to enjoy. In fact, though some children are too depressed even to describe their apathy, their family and teachers can usually see it.

Younger children lose interest in play. They're not particularly attracted to or curious about new toys, they shy away from playful peers, and they just don't seem to have fun. Some can't even listen to their mother read a story from beginning to end. Sally, 7, said, "I don't want to talk with anyone, or be with anyone. . . . I don't want to have fun; I don't think I even could."

Social withdrawal typically marks adolescent depression. Since peer relationships are so important for most teenagers, something is usually seriously wrong when they don't want to be with friends.

Before she became depressed, Marie had been the hub of the freshman class social network. All the arrangements and most of the phone calls radiated from her. In fact, Marie's parents had been perturbed that their daughter could scarcely find time for homework because she was so involved with her friends.

Then the tide turned. No one could remember which happened first, whether Marie got depressed and then lost her friends, or whether she fell from favor with the in-crowd and then got depressed. But suddenly the calls and weekend social plans disappeared.

When I saw her, Marie had completely lost interest in her former friends, whom she described as shallow. Marie's friends appeared equally uninterested in her. The girl got snubbed at school and even received some harassing phone calls.

But when her thin veneer of unconcern cracked, Marie broke down and cried about how terribly rejected she felt. She expressed anger at friends she deemed disloyal, but she blamed herself more than anyone else. Marie now felt as if she'd been an impostor, someone who had only pretended to be smooth, self-confident, and popular. Now isolated, Marie concluded she was finally getting the treatment she really deserved.

Appetite Disturbance

Some depressed children show a marked increase or decrease in appetite. Your child may gain or lose a significant amount of weight, or fail to grow as expected. Eating disorders such as anorexia or bulimia can be closely associated with depression (see Chapter 5).

Of course, children's eating habits tend to be highly variable, and many do fine on portions or combinations that astound their parents. But be alert if you note a marked change in your child's eating habits, such as the disappearance of morning hunger in a child who used to relish breakfast.

Ben's mother suspected something was wrong with her 10-year-old son when the formerly enthusiastic eater began to pick at his food and leave half of each meal on his plate. Indeed, Ben's appetite mirrored his outlook on life: sluggish, uninterested, and joyless. Ben eventually thrived on a combination of therapy and antidepressant medication which restored both his mood and his appetite.

Sleep Disturbance

Your child or adolescent may have difficulty falling asleep, awaken frequently during the night, or arise too early in the morning. Or he may seem to sleep constantly.

You may or may not associate these problems with depression. Tommy, 9, began to awaken in the middle of the night to go into his parents' room. His parents suspected something was wrong, but they guessed he was simply getting used to his mother's starting work. When Tommy stopped visiting their room at night, they assumed he'd adjusted.

Indeed, once children establish independent nighttime routines, parents may well be unaware of their child's sleep difficulties. In therapy I discovered that Tommy's sleeping problems continued for weeks after he returned to his room. Tommy had stopped going into his parents' room not because he felt better, but because he'd become worried that his pet bird would be frightened if he left it alone. Back in his room, Tommy continued to wake up and often lay for hours trying to fall back asleep. But his parents never guessed.

If your child looks sleepy or complains of tiring quickly at school or play, ask him how he's sleeping at night. You might try to find out how long it takes him to fall asleep and what he thinks about when he's trying to get to sleep. Ask him whether he worries and what he worries about. Does he have bad dreams or nightmares? What are they like?

If your child dismisses your questions, you may want to check on him. Go to his room about an hour after his bedtime and see whether he's still lying awake. You might also check in the middle of the night to see whether he's restless. And if your child comes to your room in the middle of the night seeking comfort from a nightmare, ask him about it.

Research studies indicate that even when a depressed child appears to be sleeping normally and says he slept through the night, his sleep architecture may be disturbed by depression. Sleep architecture refers to how sleep patterns are organized within the brain. For example, a depressed person may have great difficulty falling asleep, and then experience a shortened period before his first dream cycle. Disturbances of sleep architecture disrupt the restfulness of sleep. So your depressed child may not be getting enough rest even if he's sleeping straight through the night.

Loss of Energy

Especially if she's not sleeping well at night, your child will probably display diminished energy during the day. You can tell if your child's energy level is flagging by comparing her activity to that of children her own age and to her own energy levels of six months or a year ago.

Does your child have trouble keeping up with other children? Does she ask to sit out a game because she's tired or doesn't feel like playing? Has her energy level fallen from what it was before? Does she play for a shorter time or ask to go home earlier? These clues all point to a decreasing energy level.

While energy depletion can signal depression, it may also represent a medical problem. In Chapter 3, we will discuss the kinds of medical problems that can mimic or accompany depression.

A Change in Activity

Your depressed child may show a general slowing of thought, speech, and movement, appearing almost sluggish. If your formerly active child sits around more, moves haltingly from place to place, and speaks sparingly or in a mono- tone, suspect depression.

On the other hand, some depressed children appear to be agitated and restless, with excess "nervous energy" they just can't seem to discharge. If your child is old enough to describe it, he may tell you he feels "tense" or "jittery" or "nervous inside."

Ron, 11, caught the attention of his teacher because he drummed his fingers on the desk and constantly shifted about in his chair. During free time, Ron wandered about the room restlessly, almost as if he were pacing. Because hyperactivity often accompanies attention deficit dis- order, Ron's teacher believed the boy might have this con- dition. But Ron had always been a calm, low-key child before this year, and attention deficit disorder usually appears earlier in life. Ron's agitation turned out to be a sign of depression.

Physical Symptoms

Symptoms such as headaches and stomachaches without identifiable physical causes often accompany depression, especially in younger children. These aches and pains come and go, and sometimes it's hard for a parent to keep track of how often a child expresses vague physical complaints. But if your child complains frequently, and your pediatrician or family doctor can find nothing physically wrong, your child may well be depressed.

The Langs brought their 11-year-old daughter, Melissa, to see me because the girl had missed over 20 days of school in the fall semester. In Melissa's case, a variety of trivial illnesses that warranted a one-day absence had stretched to three or four days or an entire week.

Mondays tended to be Melissa's worst day, with vague physical complaints beginning on Sunday night as she anticipated returning to school. In the morning, Melissa would often say she had a stomachache or headache and didn't want to go to school. Her parents vacillated, occasionally taking a firm stand and insisting that she go anyway, and at other times giving in and letting her stay home. Melissa's mother, especially, worried about forcing her daughter to go to school "if she really doesn't feel well." But Melissa's grades had plunged. She was also falling out of the social mainstream because the other students had come to view her as sickly.

When I spoke with Melissa, I discovered that she wasn't only anxious about her performance in school and her standing with her peers, she was seriously depressed as well. For months, Melissa had had difficulty concentrating on her schoolwork, remembering what the teacher said, and performing up to her own high standards. The girl reported trouble sleeping at night and loss of interest in hobbies and social activities. In fact, she said, "I'd really rather just stay home curled up in bed."

Like Felice's mother, Melissa's parents focused on their child's school problem, but they might have picked up on her social isolation, too. Melissa had stopped calling friends and no longer even made plans for the weekend. And the girl who had previously spent much of her free

time at her beloved stable had begun retiring to her room
every day after school.

Feelings of Worthlessness and Guilt

Your depressed child's sense of being worthless or feeling
guilty will be out of proportion to anything she has actually done. This feeling persists nearly every day. Low self-
esteem, another central feature of depression, rarely occurs in uncomplicated bereavement or as part of the normal ups and downs of childhood. Low self-esteem may
cause your child to make statements like these: "I can't do
anything right." "Nobody wants to be my friend." "This
family would be better off without me." "I ruin things for
everybody else."

These statements alone don't prove that your child is
depressed. But think about them in the context of everything else you've observed about your child. For example, a
young child might say on occasion, "I'm a bad girl," and
may even feel guilty about something she's done. But a
healthy child won't feel guilty every day, nor will she
display other signs of depression.

If your child says something that seems to indicate feelings of guilt or worthlessness, try to listen without correcting or denying. Find out what she feels guilty about and
whether it's rational. If your child's guilt seems irrational
or disproportionate, look for other signs of depression.

Occasionally, external events like a failing grade or an
extracurricular disappointment can make your child question her competence. But a healthy child usually has
enough self-esteem in reserve to brush it off and move on.
The depressed child or adolescent takes negative events,
even seemingly trivial ones, as evidence that she is worthless and incompetent.

Is your child a perfectionist? Some perfectionistic children set extremely high standards for themselves and find

any failure devastating. Dr. David Shaffer from Columbia University has identified a subgroup of teens who have attempted suicide. When confronted with the occasional failures that everyone encounters, these children may react with plummeting self-esteem, extreme self-criticism, and even suicide (see Chapter 7).

Your depressed child may accuse herself or put herself down. Linda, 16, said, "My friends don't understand what's going on with me, but I wouldn't expect them to. I feel as if I'm no use to anyone. I don't do anything important, anything anyone really needs. People give me a hard time, but I guess I deserve it. I can't even stick up for myself."

Depressed children typically express guilt about their relationship with their parents. A depressed child may confess, "I feel like I've done something terrible to my parents," or "I'm a constant disappointment to my parents—I'm always letting them down," or "I don't think I love my parents as much as I should."

Of course, children—and particularly adolescents— frequently express anger toward their parents. Healthy children and their parents realize that normal angry feelings can accompany tender, loving ones. But depressed children may feel guilty because they fear that their negative feelings actually harm their parents.

Your depressed child might express guilt about many other issues, from things she has done to things she has only imagined. Try to draw your child out by probing gently, being careful not to deny the validity of her feelings.

Decreased Concentration

Your depressed child may show a diminished ability to think or concentrate. He might have trouble focusing on a conversation or be unable to watch an entire television program. After paging absently through a magazine, he may remember almost nothing of what he's seen.

Because school makes so many demands on a child's concentration, your depressed child's academic performance will probably suffer. He may become so frustrated and ashamed that he becomes reluctant to attend school. One educational diagnostic unit reported that 45 percent of their cases of school refusal demonstrated significant depression (see Chapter 4).

Thoughts of Death

Recurrent thoughts of death or suicide clearly distinguish a depressive disorder from more normal transient depressions or uncomplicated bereavement. You may hear your child say things like "Life isn't worth living," "I'd be better off dead," "Sometimes I feel dead inside," or "I think my family would be better off without me."

You might be tempted to dismiss such statements because they're unbelievable; in fact, children under 12 rarely do kill themselves. But depressed children commonly *contemplate* killing themselves. You need to pay careful attention to such statements, which are red flags for depression. Listen to your child and try to find out what is making him feel so bad that death seems preferable to life (see Chapter 7).

Hopelessness

Not all depressed children feel hopeless. In other words, your child may be depressed without deciding that there's no hope of things getting better. But many depressed children have lost even the slightest hope of change.

The conviction that things will never get better causes extreme pain for the depressed child and his family.

Indeed, many experts believe hopelessness provides an especially sensitive indicator of suicide risk.

Anxiety

Symptoms of anxiety frequently accompany depression, making it difficult to determine which one is your child's primary problem. Your young child might cling to you, shadowing you wherever you go. Or he may be preoccupied with muggers and robbers, expressing concern for his own or your safety.

Older depressed children and adolescents frequently worry about things they have done in the past. They may also ruminate about how they are doing in school, about how competent they are, or about their future in general. An anxious child may seek constant reassurance and appear completely unable to relax. A competent therapist can help you determine whether your child's anxiety is contributing to his depression or whether it constitutes a separate problem.

Disturbed Interpersonal Relationships

Your depressed child may have disturbed relationships with you, with her siblings, with her peers, and with her teachers. In fact, teachers tend to complain more frequently to the parents of depressed children than they do to the parents of children who are not depressed. Depressed children don't make friends easily, can't seem to keep a "best" friend, visit friends less, and get teased more often than other children.

After treatment for depression, your child may recover her school functioning more easily than she solves her problems with friends. Treating depression in children should include attention to the relationship problems that often accompany it. Social skills not only promote recovery from depression but play a crucial role in your child's general psychological well-being.

Dreams and Fantasy

Children of all ages express fantasy, even children too young to put their thoughts and feelings clearly into words. In working with depressed children, I commonly see evidence of depression in joyless play and bleak drawings in which human figures often appear primitive or disfigured.

Your child may also express her depression through dreams or fantasies. As a parent you needn't feel obliged to analyze your child's dreams. But if she complains of a nightmare, ask what happened in her dream. If nightmares keep recurring or if your child wakes up consistently, look for the other warning signs of depression.

Younger children express fantasies in their drawings or play. You might join in the play or just comment about it, encouraging further elaboration or discussion.

Your child's fantasy themes alone don't prove she's depressed. But studies conducted by Dr. Donald McKnew found that mildly depressed children frequently repeated themes of being disappointed, thwarted, mistreated, excluded, blamed, or criticized. Their play themes and drawings included being lost, ridiculed, rejected, or physically injured. Deeply depressed children portrayed the subjects of suicide, being killed or mutilated, or losing a loved one.

Depressed adolescents, especially creative ones, may produce art or poetry that offers an articulate expression of their experience. They may also describe daydreams in which they imagine themselves getting hurt or killed.

Hallucinations and Delusions

Your depressed child may hear voices telling him he is bad or worthless, or even telling him to kill himself. Many children, especially younger ones, will talk about the voices they hear or delusional ideas they believe. Patti, 9, for example, believed her dead grandmother came to life at night in a trunk at the foot of her bed. Not surprisingly, she was afraid of going to sleep and she awoke in terror in the middle of the night.

Since older children and adolescents fear social stigma, they may try valiantly to hide this symptom. One mother became alarmed when she heard her teenage son engaged in a heated argument while he was alone in the backyard. Her son denied that he'd been talking to anyone. But he eventually needed to be hospitalized with a major depression.

Your depressed child or adolescent may experience delusional thinking—false beliefs based on incorrect interpretations of reality. Typically, children's delusions relate to unforgivable moral failure, sexual misconduct, persecution for imagined deficiencies, or fears of severe punishment.

DEPRESSED CHILDREN AND DEPRESSED ADOLESCENTS

Depression looks very different in children of different ages. A young child may appear sad and cry much of the time. He may be quite easily frustrated, getting mad and staying mad for a long time. Depressed preschoolers frequently claim that they like to tease other children and make them feel bad. Unable to describe his mood, your young child might say that he feels "tired" or that he can't keep up with his friends.

An older child or adolescent, on the other hand, can more easily reflect on his own feelings and describe them to you, if he chooses to do so. In trying to determine whether your older child is depressed, you won't have to rely so much on observations about his moods from play or behavior.

Younger children may appear more visibly depressed than adolescents and experience more physical complaints, behavioral agitation, phobias, hallucinations, and anxiety about separation from their parents. Adolescents tend to express more hopelessness, blunted feelings, excessive sleeping, weight changes, and use of alcohol and illicit drugs. Depressed children think about suicide as much as adolescents do, but their attempts are much less likely to be as life-threatening.

But despite obvious differences in their ability to express their feelings, depressed young children and adolescents share many of the same symptoms. In fact, researchers found almost no differences between the two groups on the vast majority of depressive signs. Most of the differences they detailed merely related to the greater independence adolescents enjoy.

BIPOLAR DISORDER

In bipolar disorder, depression alternates with its opposite, mania. Mania usually declares itself with an elevated or excessively irritable mood, increased physical activity, a decreased need for sleep, and grandiose thinking.

Extremely rare in children, bipolar disorder occasionally makes its first appearance before age 20. The disease typically recurs, with 50 to 90 percent of bipolar patients experiencing multiple episodes. The duration of each episode and the length of cycles vary, but the average manic episode lasts three months and the average depressive episode lasts between four and six months.

MANIC SYMPTOMS IN CHILDREN OR ADOLESCENTS

- Drastic changes in mood, such as extreme elation or silliness, or intense irritability
- Exaggerated self-esteem or grandiosity: the conviction that one has the power to save the world
- Sudden unnatural increase in energy: going without sleep for days without feeling tired or slowing down
- Excessive talkativeness: rapid, uninterruptible speech; jumping from one topic to another
- Marked distractibility: easily diverted attention
- High-risk behavior: reckless driving and other dangerous actions

John, 16, attended an urban "magnet school" that drew gifted students from all over the city. Bright enough to do well in every subject, John had a special interest in writing and had won numerous academic prizes for his literary efforts.

During the fall semester of his junior year, John piled two extra courses on top of his already heavy course load and insisted on joining every extracurricular activity he could find because they would look good on his college applications. The boy pursued an elaborate schedule that included his many activities, two to three hours a day for homework, and a strict ritual of exercise.

At first, John maintained his usual good grades, but by late October, his essays had begun to come back with grades of C or D. John's surprised teachers wrote comments such as "illogical arguments" and "this essay has nothing to do with the assignment." In class, John was beginning to act strangely, too, rambling on about unrelated topics in a class discussion or lashing out at a classmate who disagreed with his opinion.

Even John's friends began to be concerned. John's best friend could not understand why John was calling his house all night, waking him and his family up to talk about "nonsense." Another group of friends brought John home early on a Saturday night because he was "acting weird and getting into fights." Although John had always been staunchly against drugs, his friends concluded that he might have taken something.

Nailing blankets and shower curtains over all his windows to "escape the tyranny of circadian rhythms," John finally stopped sleeping completely. After he stayed up three nights in a row writing incomprehensible poetry, John's bewildered parents brought him to the emergency room in an acutely agitated state.

When I first met John, he was pacing restlessly and talking in an endless stream of imagery and pseudophilosophical nonsense. Instead of responding to any of my questions directly, John sought to explain to me how colors could be used as an alphabet to build a powerful new language. When I told John he needed to be admitted to the hospital for evaluation and treatment, he suddenly became hostile and demanded to be allowed to leave so he could get on with his important mission.

For nearly a week, John proved extremely difficult to manage. He flooded the bathroom floor twice, tried to escape through the ceiling, and kept other patients up most of the night. Medication to dampen his psychosis, relieve his agitation, and allow sleep didn't take effect for several days.

For their part, John's parents were in a state of shock. Like John's friends, they had assumed he must have been having some sort of drug reaction. But all of John's drug tests came back negative. Indeed, a careful history revealed that John suffered from bipolar disorder, commonly called manic-depression.

Treatment for Bipolar Disorder

People with bipolar disorder usually receive antipsychotic medication to interrupt the acute manic episode. If your child's diagnosis turns out to be bipolar disorder, he may receive the drug lithium to minimize recurrences (see Chapter 9).

But like any other mental disorder in a child, bipolar illness should be treated with a multimodal approach. You and your child will need education about the nature and course of the illness. Individual therapy can help your child make personal changes to alleviate stress and decrease the likelihood of recurrences. Family therapy will improve communication within your family, help you support your child, and enable you to deal with your own reactions to the illness (see Chapter 9).

A FINAL WORD

Is your child depressed? If several of the symptoms just described cluster together in your child, if they are serious enough to be noticeable to her or to you, and if they persist for more than a few days, your child may indeed be clinically depressed. These symptoms should alert you to seek professional evaluation and treatment for your child.

But throughout this process, don't think of your child as just a bundle of symptoms and problems. Indeed, as you begin to observe your child and become more sensitive to her, you will realize that she has many more strengths than she has symptoms. In the chapters to come, where we focus more on what you can do about your child's depression, we'll detail how you can help your child develop those strengths. With your help, she'll grow in skill, in confidence, and in self-esteem.

3

WHY IS YOUR CHILD DEPRESSED?

When your child experiences a serious illness such as depression, you want to know why it happened. You may speculate, "It was probably the divorce," or "Maybe we shouldn't have moved," or "He's just like my Great Uncle Harry." The fact is, it's often impossible to tell.

As you read through this chapter, you will encounter a variety of interesting theories, some of which may seem to "explain" your child's case. You will also find many helpful suggestions to protect your child against a recurrence. But most likely you will never learn exactly what caused his depression. Despite recent advances in our understanding of this illness, researchers have found no single explanation that can account for childhood depression.

A DELICATE BALANCE

Consider your child's depression the way you would any illness. Illness usually strikes when a person's normal balance gets disrupted. Balance, of course, involves a combination

43

of inside and outside factors. If you catch a cold, for example, it may be that the cold virus took hold because you were run-down from lack of sleep. Had you been in better condition, the virus, might not have found such a welcoming environment. Or, conversely, if you had not been exposed to the virus your run-down state might not have mattered. To figure out why you got sick at this particular time, you'd have to consider both internal vulnerability and an external stress or trigger.

The general principle applies to depression. A child who becomes clinically depressed probably carries a combination of genetic, psychological, and environmental risk factors that makes him especially vulnerable to life's many stresses.

On the opposite side of the balance, your child's strengths—genetic, psychological, and environmental— usually help to keep him well. Depression strikes when something happens that shifts this delicate balance. That "something" may be physical (the onset of puberty or a major illness), psychological (a real or perceived deprivation, such as losing a friend or relative), or environmental (perhaps failing a course in school). The more vulnerable your child, the less severe the stressor will have to be to tip him off balance. Conversely, the more protective factors he has, the less vulnerable he will be to depression under stress.

You've probably noticed that some people seem to get more colds than others. Perhaps you're one of them. If so, you know you have to pay special attention to staying healthy. Likewise, you will want to pay special attention to promoting the strengths that can restore a healthy balance for your depressed child. Just as you might try to minimize the severity of a cold by taking vitamin C and drinking chicken soup, you can help tilt your depressed child's scale back toward equilibrium in many important ways.

So as you read about the risks and stresses that may contribute to a child's depression, remember that your child's illness does not represent his eventual destiny, but rather a temporary aberration. Keep in mind, too, that restoring a balance between risk, stressful life events, and protective strengths can help preserve your child's future health.

A famous research study demonstrated the important role a healthy balance plays in maintaining a child's well-being. In 1954, psychologist Emmy Werner and several of her colleagues began a detailed investigation of the families of all the children who would be born on the Hawaiian island of Kauai in 1955. These 698 children were assessed at birth, at 1 year of age, and again when they were 2, 10, and 18 years old. The children of Kauai grew up in poor homes, and many were exposed to stressful life events. Yet some of the most stressed children developed surprisingly well, a quality Werner and Ruth Smith termed "resilience" in their book *Vulnerable but Invincible* (McGraw-Hill, 1982).

Werner and Smith described the sources of risk and stress that made some of the children of Kauai especially vulnerable to problems. Then they outlined the constitutional strengths and community supports that allowed some children to thrive in spite of their stressful childhoods.

Not surprisingly, children at the highest risk grew up in homes plagued by poverty, lack of education, and parental mental illness. Complications at birth, developmental problems, and genetic abnormalities all added further hazard. Life stresses that threatened the Kauai children included separation from a primary caretaker in the first year of life, the birth of a younger sibling in less than two years, serious or repeated childhood illnesses, parental illness, a handicapped sibling, chronic family discord, an absent father, job loss or sporadic parental employment, change of residence, change of school, parents' divorce, a parent's remarriage and the entry of a stepparent into household, the departure or death of an older sibling or close friend, and foster home placement.

Constitutional strengths and community supports weighed in on the positive side of the balance. In the cases of children

Emmy Werner and Ruth Smith termed "resilient," these pluses helped maintain health even in the most vulnerable and stressed families. Personal features that stacked the deck in a child's favor included the following: an intact central nervous system; a high activity level; a good-natured disposition; a lack of distressing habits; autonomy, as evidenced by advanced self-help abilities; adequate communication skills; the ability to focus attention and control impulses; special interests and hobbies; positive self-concept; internal locus of control (see pp. 58–59); and the desire for self-improvement.

The following family and community elements also played a role in protecting a child from stress: being the firstborn; four or fewer siblings, spaced more than two years apart; much attention paid to the infant in his first year; a positive parent-child relationship in early childhood; additional caretakers besides the mother; care by siblings and grandparents; the availability of relatives, neighbors, teachers, and ministers; structure and rules in the household; shared values; close peer friends; and access to health, education, and social services.

In the rest of this chapter, we will consider risk and stress factors in greater detail. Risks and stresses represent those elements in your child's genes and in his life that may make him particularly vulnerable to becoming depressed. Then we will examine several theories that offer interesting perspectives on childhood depression, even though no one theory completely explains the phenomenon. Throughout the chapter we will begin to identify some of the internal and environmental strengths that can help tip your child back into a healthy balance.

GENETIC RISK FACTORS

Even though your child didn't inherit depression the way she may have inherited your dark hair or your spouse's freckles, the illness does seem to run in families. Perhaps the clearest indication of this comes from studies of twins. Such studies suggest how much of any feature may be genetically determined. Since identical, or monozygotic, twins have identical genes, they are much more likely to share genetically related illnesses than are fraternal, or dizygotic, twins, who are no more closely related than any two siblings.

When researchers have studied twin pairs in which one twin suffered manic-depressive illness, they found the same illness in two-thirds of the identical-twin partners. Fraternal twins of manic-depressives had only a 14 percent likelihood of sharing this illness.

Environment is important, too. Identical twins reared together are significantly more likely to both show depression (76 percent) than are identical twins who grow up apart (67 percent). But genes definitely matter. Even when reared apart, identical twins share depression much more frequently than do fraternal twins reared together (19 percent).

Researchers have also attempted to tease out hereditary from environmental factors by studying children who were adopted away from their biological parents. They reason that if genetic factors predominate, adoptees will more likely share the illness of their biological parents. But if environmental factors predominate, the children will more closely resemble their adoptive parents.

Depression, especially bipolar disorder, certainly appears to carry a strong genetic link. In a group of adopted people suffering from manic-depression, 31 percent of their biological parents shared the illness compared to only 2 percent of the adoptive parents.

Scientists call this genetic propensity to an illness "genetic loading." It's as if a child had inherited a loaded pair of dice. Perhaps not surprisingly, genetic loading appears to be greatest in the very few children who show the symptoms of manic-depression before they reach puberty.

As many as 30 percent of these children's relatives also suffer from manic-depression. But if manic-depression first strikes a child in adolescence, fewer than 1 in 10 of his relatives will share the diagnosis.

Many studies have shown that a child with one depressed parent has a 1-in-4 chance of suffering depression at some time during life. But if both parents are depressed, a child has more than a 50-50 chance of being affected.

Studies of the children of depressed parents, however, cannot separate the effects of genetic loading from environmental stresses. Not only does the child of a depressed parent inherit a genetic susceptibility, she must also be influenced by growing up in a depressive environment.

ENVIRONMENTAL STRESS FACTORS

Having a Depressed Parent

Not surprisingly, acute or chronic depression seriously limits a person's ability to be an involved mother or father. A depressed parent may be unable to play with or even to take adequate care of a young child. When the child grows older, the depressed parent may be unaware of the child's school activities, social life, friends, and interests. The depressed parent of a teenager probably has little energy available to set appropriate limits or to encourage healthy activities. Indeed, depressed parents report that they feel less affection for their children than other parents do for theirs.

How does the child of a depressed parent respond? Children have said that they have felt guilty or responsible, as though it were their fault that their parent was sick. Some have felt obliged to take care of a depressed parent, to protect the parent by being perfect or by hiding or denying their own problems.

Feminist writer Gloria Steinem, for example, spent her childhood taking care of a mother who suffered from severe episodes of depression. In *Revolution from Within* (Little, Brown, 1992), Steinem recalls:

> Since I always knew my parents were doing the best they could, I didn't allow myself to be angry—and thus just buried my feelings about what I had missed. . . . I remember feeling sad about navigating life by myself, working after school, worrying about my mother, who was sometimes too removed from reality to know where she was, or who I was, and concealing these shameful family secrets from my friends . . .

Another child might become more demanding, trying to force her withdrawn parent to respond, even negatively.

Of course, children learn primarily by imitating their parents. In many cases, children seem to "learn" a depressed style from their parents.

But each child's response is different. One child might withdraw from her friends or family and become a virtual recluse. Another may rebel, angrily distancing herself from her parent's problems. Either of these reactions could ultimately swamp a vulnerable child with guilt for turning away from her helpless parent.

Infants and young children whose parents suffer from depression seem to have more trouble attaching themselves to their parents and to other adults. Researchers have noted that these children's relationships are marked by conflict, instability, and dissatisfaction. They show early difficulties in handling negative emotions like sadness and anger, and they find it hard to maintain an even emotional keel.

Certainly not all depressed parents have depressed children, and not all depressed children have depressed parents. But children of depressed parents do carry an increased risk for depression on several counts: First, they bear a genetic load, perhaps in the form of inherited traits that make them more vulnerable to depression. Second, they grow up under the care of someone who is emotionally if not physically unavailable, so they may not be getting all the love and support they need. Finally, as they grow up, they may be watching and imitating depressive behaviors.

In a recent study of the adolescent children of mentally ill parents, researchers found that children who excelled shared several important qualities: self-understanding, problem-solving ability, commitment to relationships, an orientation to action, and the ability to think and act separately from their parents. Not surprisingly, it helped, too, if these children had one healthy parent.

Other Life Stresses

Besides a depressed parent, several other stresses appear consistently in the histories of depressed children. For some children, physical insults such as serious illness, chronic pain, or disfigurement seem to contribute to the origin of the depression.

For other children, emotional stresses play a larger role. In many cases, depressed children report experiencing separation from important people, especially in the first few years of life. Some depressed children have been utterly rejected by their parents or caretakers. Years of repeated criticism or humiliation can send the unmistakable message that a child is incompetent. Overprotection conveys the same message, because it undermines the child's ability to cope independently.

Depressed children also seem to have experienced more than their share of family losses, though not always through death. A loved person may not be there physically or emotionally, because he or she is ill, divorced, traveling, moved, or involved with others. This stress seems to be particularly traumatic if the child depended on the loved one before the loss and if no appropriate substitute took over afterward.

Societal Stresses

To account for the recent upsurge in the number of children seeking psychiatric help for depression, researchers have suggested several cultural catalysts: urbanization and suburbanization, the disintegration of the extended family, geographic mobility, altered family structures, more single and working mothers, and occupational shifts.

The nuclear family has undergone a radical transformation in the last few decades. Only 12 percent of the nation's children lived in single-parent households in 1970; 25 percent did in 1991.

Changes in family structure, in the economy, and in educational opportunities for women have sent many more mothers to work, leaving children in day care or with substitute caregivers. In 1960, 20 percent of mothers with children under 6 years old worked outside the home. By 1991, that figure had almost tripled to 58 percent, and the majority of employed mothers were working full time.

The sluggish economy of the early 1990s widened the gap between rich and poor, even as divorce disrupted family attachments and geographic mobility decreased the support of the extended family. In my own practice, more parents than not answer "No one" when I ask who they can rely on for help and advice. More parents than ever seem to feel that they live in what one father aptly termed "high-anxiety zip codes."

Some theorists even go so far as to suggest that childhood depression can result solely from outside stresses, changes, or traumas. Indeed, depressed children *have* experienced more than their share of moves, parental job losses and financial strain, marital discord, and school difficulties.

But the life stress model can never fully explain childhood depression, because, as the Kauai study demonstrated, many children who appear to be extraordinarily stressed from the outside never become depressed. And a fair number of children become clinically depressed without any obvious life stressors at all. And even the normal, predictable events in a child's life cycle—going to school for the first time, for example—may be quite stressful. Not surprisingly, the very steep rise in life stresses at the beginning of adolescence coincides with a corresponding rise in the frequency of depression.

Since stress can play a major role in depression, however, you should watch for it in your family and make the attempt to minimize it. Institute regimens such as regular exercise and good nutrition that can reduce stress. Your children will not automatically become depressed when life stresses occur, but try to be particularly alert when a stressful event such as a job change or a move does become necessary.

OTHER THEORIES ABOUT CHILDHOOD DEPRESSION

Although no one theory can completely explain depression, you may find it instructive to examine the problem from several points of view. Since depression itself tends to narrow thinking and limit alternatives, looking at your child's illness from different perspectives can be a therapeutic exercise in itself.

Psychoanalytic Contributions

Sigmund Freud proposed the earliest theory of depression. The father of psychoanalysis speculated that depression stemmed from the real or imagined loss of a loved person. To avoid feeling angry at the lost person, the bereft person directed the anger against himself, and felt a profound sadness. According to Freud's theory, depression could be triggered by the death of a parent, the loss of health due to a serious illness, moving away from loved relatives or friends, or even the imagined or believed loss of an important relationship.

Other writers expanded on Freud's theories or studied different groups. Rene Spitz and John Bowlby, for example, looked at depressed infants. In their "object loss" model, Spitz and Bowlby argued that separation and disruption of the attachment bond precipitated depression.

Edith Jacobson argued that depression resulted from the discrepancy between a person's actual self-appraisal and his ideal self, which this psychoanalyst termed his "ego ideal." Depression, Jacobson thought, meant that a person felt incapable of becoming his ideal self. Other analytic thinkers considered depression to be a basic negative emotion, much like anxiety, that arose whenever a person lost a former state of well-being.

Historically interesting in themselves, psychoanalytic themes still play a central role in current theories about depression. Even a clinician who believes that biology is central to depression must still be struck by how frequently themes of loss and threatened self-esteem appear in the stories of depressed children.

Thanks to psychoanalytic theory, too, we have been prompted to look at internal risks and stresses. In psychoanalysis, fantasies can be just as important as actual events, depending on how the person perceives them. So we can't simply look at a child's life from the outside and add up what *we* judge to be his stresses to decide whether the child "deserves" to be depressed.

This point often proves difficult for parents to understand. They may feel, for example, that since it doesn't "really" matter if a particular boy stops liking their daughter, this shouldn't have anything to do with her self-image. In their eyes, of course, she's just as wonderful as ever. In the girl's mind, however, the event feels like a devastating rejection. As a result, the girl may conclude that she is completely undesirable and will never recover.

In other words, some of the factors that have contributed to your child's depression may not be apparent to you. Inside your child's memory lie unseen fears, fantasies, and beliefs that can affect her equilibrium. These features may well remain invisible until a sensitive therapist can help your child explore her own unique view of the world.

Cognitive Theory

Whereas Freudians maintain that depressed feelings produce negative and distorted thinking, cognitive theorists such as Drs. Aaron Beck and David Burns contend that the opposite actually occurs: that distorted thinking—specifically, negative views of one's self, one's future, and the world—produces depression.

Depressed children, cognitive theorists contend, think they are inadequate, worthless, or defective. To these children the world is a perpetually frustrating and withholding environment that makes impossible demands. The future appears to promise nothing except failure, suffering, and more hopelessness. Cognitive therapy consists of correcting children's negative thinking habits, and consequently reducing their depressed feelings.

Learning Theory

In learning theory, behaviors that don't elicit reinforcement or reward tend to fade away, while actions that elicit reinforcement increase. Reinforcement might be something as simple as smiling back when your infant smiles at you or reacting with enthusiasm to the initial babblings of a cooing baby.

Learning theory suggests that a child becomes depressed when he gets insufficient reinforcement from his environment and the people around him. The person who normally provided reinforcement may suddenly have become unavailable because of death, divorce, or her own depression.

Or perhaps the depressed child himself lacks the basic skills to elicit reinforcement. In fact, peers *have* rated depressed children as less popular, suggesting that these children actually do receive less positive feedback from others.

According to Peter Lewinsohn, a social learning theorist, a child's environment provokes depression by supplying a low rate of positive reinforcement for normal behaviors and a high rate of reinforcement for depressive behaviors. Indeed, children who exhibit depressive behaviors such as physical complaints or suicide threats usually do get the reinforcement of attention, thereby perpetuating their depression.

Of course, learning doesn't take place only at home. For older children, the social world proves equally important. In the Kauai study, a child's ability to make and keep friends served as one of the best protections against depression. Indeed, even among depressed children, those who are more isolated and unpopular have a worse prognosis.

That fact helps to explain why losing a friend can be so tragic for a child. A best friend offers approval, positive regard, and even comfort. Children frequently develop a clinical depression after they've lost a best friend because one or the other moved away, or worse, they had a falling out. In these cases, the loss seems clearly to have tipped the child's balance.

As you consider the importance of positive and negative reinforcement on your own child's self-esteem, think for a moment about her daily activities. Your child may spend 20 out of 24 hours each day in school, watching television, and sleeping. If your child is not a good student, she may not receive much positive reinforcement in school. She certainly won't get any from the three to five hours many children spend in front of the television each day. Like all of us, children need positive reinforcement, to be appreciated for what they can do well. But to get this they need to *do* something well.

Think, too, about the effects of your behavior on your child's attitudes, actions, and feelings. Make a scrupulous attempt to avoid reinforcing unhealthy or depressive behaviors like staying home from school with stomachaches or shunning friends. And provide lots of reinforcement for your child's healthy behaviors: cooperative social play among toddlers, creative pursuits among middle-schoolers, and athletics or other activities for teenagers.

Therapy based primarily on learning theory seeks to focus on helping the child develop the social skills she needs to draw more positive reinforcement from those around her. But whatever their orientation, most therapists use some elements of learning theory in their therapy for depressed children (see Chapter 9).

Aside from its contributions to therapy, learning theory has also provided us with crucial insights about childhood depression, notably the hypotheses of learned helplessness and locus of control.

LEARNED HELPLESSNESS   The idea that depression results from "learned helplessness" originated from animal experiments in the 1960s in which normal dogs at first attempted to avoid the painful stimuli of electric shocks. When the experimental animals discovered they couldn't escape from the shocks, they eventually gave up trying. Not only that, when the previously shocked animals were later put into a situation from which they *could* get away, they no longer even tried.

This motivational deficit compounded the cognitive deficiency: the dogs couldn't seem to learn new responses to avoid the shocks. They seemed depressed and hopeless as well. Lying down, passively accepting the shocks, these animals had simply given up trying. They had learned to be helpless.

In human studies, scientists found that people, too, could be "trained" to be helpless in unpleasant situations. Volunteers in the experiment who were subjected to irritating stimuli such as foul odors, loud noises, or harsh criticism lost their motivation and ability to solve problems. They soon began to expect to fail, and their self-esteem plummeted as they felt increasingly ineffective.

A child may indeed learn helplessness from repeated experiences of abuse or neglect over which he has no control. A child who is chronically subjected to physical pain, intimidation, or indifference understandably begins to expect to be treated badly. Such a child may come to believe that bad things are much more likely to happen than good ones. Even worse, if nothing he can do—pleading, apologizing, hiding, fighting back—forestalls the next punishment, a child will learn that his actions are futile. According to the theory of learned helplessness, the more a child expects something terrible to happen and the more he's convinced that there's nothing he can do about it, the more depressed he'll be.

Later researchers qualified the theory of learned helplessness by demonstrating the importance of a person's *attributions* about the uncontrollable events. Attributions may be internal or external, stable or variable, and global or specific.

For example, if someone attributes negative events to internal characteristics—"Mother got sick and died because I didn't take good enough care of her"—rather than external ones—"Mother got sick and died because she was weak and elderly and was exposed to a virulent pneumonia"—depression will be more likely to accompany the sense of helplessness.

If a person attributes negative events to stable factors that persist over time—"I have always been unable to help my loved ones when they need it and I'll never be any better"—rather than variable ones—"It was a bad time for me at work and I wasn't available to my mother as much as

I would have liked"—then helplessness increases and depression follows.

If someone believes his shortcoming to be global rather than specific—"I'm too selfish to be of help to anyone, anytime," rather than "I was self-absorbed at that time, but there were other times when I was a good son"—then depression is more likely.

As researchers at the University of Pennsylvania predicted, children who attributed *bad* events to internal, stable, and global causes ("My friend Johnny refused to play with me because I'm a totally boring person") instead of external, variable, specific causes ("My friend Johnny refused to play with me because he's having a bad day, but he'll probably get over it, and he might be more interested if I suggest we shoot baskets instead of going swimming") were at greater risk for depression.

In addition, these high-risk children also tended to attribute *good* events to external, variable, and specific causes ("She just called me up because she needs someone to do the homework for her"). Their mothers, though not their fathers, shared some of these attributional styles, suggesting that, like helplessness, these features may be learned and subject to therapeutic change.

Learned helplessness aptly describes the attitudes of many depressed children and can play a crucial role in education and therapy. As a parent, you'll want to try to teach your children the sense of effectiveness that comes from the inside. This conviction can help immunize your child against depression when life's stresses strike. If your child tends to blame himself for every failure and attribute all his successes to luck, help him recognize how events really happen and show him how to take action on his own behalf.

LOCUS OF CONTROL   Social learning theory also gives us the concept of locus of control. This term refers to the extent to which a person believes she personally controls the environment around her. A person with an external locus of control feels that factors outside herself—luck, chance, the actions of others—largely determine what happens in her life. Someone with an internal locus of control, on the other hand, believes that her own actions exert a positive impact on the course of events around her.

Attribution theory and locus of control are related but not identical concepts. Attribution has to do with assigning meaning to events. The depressive pattern is to attribute positive events to external causes and negative events to internal, stable, and global causes. Locus of control, on the other hand, refers to a sense of efficacy over events. A depressed person feels as though power resides outside himself (external locus of control), while a normal person feels as though he has authority over most things in his life (internal locus of control).

Research shows that academic confidence, social maturity, independence, striving, self-motivation, and success all correlate to a child's having an internal locus of control. Not surprisingly, children with chronic illnesses such as diabetes or inflammatory bowel disease often have a relatively external locus of control. How well they can gain an internal locus of control often predicts how well their disease can be managed.

Biological Theories

Because dramatic advances in understanding the biology of depression have led to effective new drug treatments, you may wonder whether your child has a "biochemical imbalance" or a "biochemical depression." Biological theories certainly seem more concrete and more scientific than psychoanalytic and learning theories, with their abstract concepts of "object loss" and "locus of control." In fact, biological explanations appear to bring the problem of depression into the realm of other medical conditions, illnesses for which you can just go to a doctor and get a pill. Many patients feel reassured that a simple answer finally exists to a problem that has been so baffling and worrisome.

But despite all we have discovered recently, no single medical theory can explain depression, and no simple cure exists. Certain medications may be very effective in treating depression (see Chapter 9), but even these don't offer a total solution. The less tangible psychological aspects of the problem still demand our therapeutic attention.

Bear in mind, too, that research findings on depressed adults may not be completely applicable to depressed children. Because the neurotransmitter system changes when the central nervous system has matured, children cannot simply be considered miniature adults. With these important caveats in mind, your child's depression may well have a biological component.

DISEASES THAT CAN CAUSE OR MIMIC DEPRESSION   Certain physical conditions can actually produce depression or imitate it so well that you should certainly have your depressed child thoroughly examined by a physician to rule out a medical disorder. In some cases, treating the medical condition that has brought about a depression will relieve the depression as well.

The chart on page 61 shows a list of illnesses and medications that can cause or mimic depression in children and adolescents. While some of these illnesses are extremely rare, others occur much more commonly. Likewise, some of these diseases are accompanied by depression only rarely, others more frequently.

As you look at the chart, don't worry that your depressed child may have some exotic or fatal illness. Most likely, he doesn't. But your child's medical doctor should evaluate him to rule out these physical illnesses.

Illness	Test(s)
anemia	complete blood count with differential
infections	complete blood count with differential
endocrine disorders	blood chemistries: electrolytes, blood sugar, BUN, creatinine, and liver enzymes
thyroid diseases	thyroid function tests
seizures	electroencephalogram (EEG)
brain tumors	CAT scan

BIOCHEMICAL IMBALANCES A spate of recent research suggests that depressed people lack adequate stores of certain neurotransmitters such as norepinephrine and serotonin. These naturally occurring brain chemicals serve as chemical messengers in the brain and regulate such states as a person's mood.

Like depressed adults, depressed children tend to excrete significantly less urinary MHPG, the main metabolite of brain norepinephrine, than well children do. In adult depression this finding has prompted the use of antidepressant medication, significantly increasing available neurotransmitters in the brain and thereby relieving symptoms.

People with a mood disorder may also have abnormalities in their brain system that includes the pituitary gland and the hypothalamus. Depressed adults and children, for example, both show irregularities in the pituitary gland's secretion of growth hormone.

In depressed adults and children, the adrenal gland appears to oversecrete cortisol. This hormone is essential in small amounts to regulate the body's ability to cope with stress. The fact that many depressed patients produce excess cortisol provides one of the more common biological tests for depression, the dexamethasone suppression test (DST).

Here's how the DST works. A "suppressing" dose of the steroid dexamethasone is given to a patient. Normally a person responds by shutting down his own production of cortisol for 12 to 24 hours, since the drug provides plenty. But depressed patients fail to suppress their own cortisol production. Their surplus production of this hormone can be detected with a blood test. A positive DST suggests a major depression.

About 70 percent of prepubertal children with a major depression will test positive on the DST. The test has proven less sensitive with depressed adolescents, however. Only about half of severely depressed adolescents have a positive DST, probably because of the vast hormonal changes they are undergoing.

BIORHYTHMIC DISORDERS   Most of us are familiar with the common daily rhythms such as sleeping-waking cycles and the body temperature cycles that make us coolest during the early morning hours. People are also subject to rhythms that extend across several days or weeks, most notably a woman's menstrual cycles.

Interesting research on psychobiological mood rhythms shows predictable variations across a day throughout the life cycle. Older people, for example, report feeling consistently better in the morning than they do in the evening. Younger people, on the other hand, typically report feeling worse in the morning and better later in the day. Studies also show something that would surprise no parent of a teenager: Adolescents normally show much wider and more rapid mood variations than adults do.

Two categories of depression, known by their acronyms SAD and PMS, may be caused by disturbances in the body's basic biorhythms. Both predominate in adults, but both SAD and PMS may be seen in children as young as 8 or 9 years old.

SAD   An estimated 10 million Americans suffer the most severe effects of the aptly abbreviated seasonal affective disorder. In SAD, depressive symptoms occur regularly in a seasonal pattern, usually appearing as the days grow short in winter and disappearing with the return of sunlight in the spring. A simple treatment—very bright light—often relieves the symptoms within days.

For example, every year around November, Lisa, 16, had showed the same pattern: school problems, sleepiness, sadness, irritability, and difficulty concentrating. Just six hours of light treatment over three days allowed her to perk up visibly. Her depressive symptoms completely disappeared, an amazing transformation that prompted her friends to be concerned that she might be on drugs. Lisa and thousands of other people who share her condition use phototherapy successfully each winter to counter the symptoms of SAD. See the Resources section for more information on seasonal affective disorder.

PMS The cyclical flux of female reproductive hormones causes an estimated 80 percent of women to experience occasional symptoms of premenstrual syndrome (PMS), including depression, irritability, tension, headache, fatigue, breast swelling and tenderness, abdominal bloating, weight gain, increased thirst or appetite, cravings for sweet or salty foods, acne, asthma, or constipation. In some women, PMS can lead to serious psychopathology.

Since PMS may strike first in preadolescence, even before puberty, take note if your otherwise normal daughter periodically shows marked changes in her mood or reactions a few days each month. PMS can be managed with diet, vitamins, exercise, stress reduction, and occasionally with progesterone therapy, but it's crucial to choose a medical specialist who is familiar with the problem. For more information on PMS, see the Resources section.

In most cases, depression results from several factors and represents an imbalance between a child's risks and stresses on one side and protective factors on the other. With information, you can help reduce your child's stresses as you build the kind of strengths that can protect her. You'll learn more about what you and the professionals can do to help your depressed child in the succeeding chapters.

If your child is depressed, insist on a thorough evaluation of physical as well as psychological causes. Don't be surprised, however, if you never get an answer to the question "Why is my child depressed?" If you're frustrated about the lack of a definitive answer, remember the advice of one determined father: "Not every problem can be completely understood or completely solved, but every problem can certainly be managed."

The Many Masks
of Childhood
Depression

4

CHILDHOOD DEPRESSION AND SCHOOL FAILURE

—

Mrs. O'Connor called me because she was concerned about Peggy, an 8-year-old she had taught for almost two years. "She seems to be losing interest in school altogether, almost as if she's disengaging. She comes in without her homework, looking blank, and then she'll say in a monotone that she 'forgot.' This year, Peggy gives up immediately on anything that challenges her. In fact, she hardly persists even on routine exercises. Do you think she could be depressed?"

When I saw Peggy, the little girl said: "I don't like school because I'm not smart. I feel bad when I'm in school except for lunch and recess. I like lunch and recess because there's no reading."

Mrs. O'Connor was right. Peggy was depressed and, sooner or later, it was bound to show up in school. For Peggy and other depressed children, school becomes a place of humiliation and pain. Depression can make a child feel incompetent, inadequate, and dumb. It can also actually impair a child's thinking and learning abilities. Despite a kind and concerned teacher like Mrs. O'Connor, Peggy's depression rendered her inadequate to the task at hand.

To function at school, your child needs to perform almost automatically a number of cognitive operations that begin with paying attention. She must focus intently to get information from a teacher or a book. Once your child receives information through her eyes or ears, she must process that information and integrate it with other information already stored in her brain. She must then compare and contrast, recognize and question inconsistencies, make mental corrections, and store the new information in her memory. Your child may need to use stored information to formulate an idea or to answer a question. This involves putting an idea into words.

Any of these cognitive functions can be affected by depression. Attention and concentration usually suffer the most. As your child becomes absorbed in her own internal sadness, she has less attention left to pay to her teacher. Depression slows and distorts information processing, so a depressed child may have trouble understanding new concepts and solving problems.

Your depressed child may also be fatigued from lack of sleep. Fatigue further undermines thinking. Since depression affects memory, your depressed child may be unable to store new information or to retrieve what she already knows.

WARNING SIGNS IN THE CLASSROOM

Like Mrs. O'Connor, your child's teacher might be the first person to notice your child's depression. If your child shows the following symptoms in school, he should be professionally evaluated for depression.

Mood Changes

Unlike anxiety disorders, psychotic disorders, and organic disorders, depression is a mood disorder. "Mood" refers to a prolonged emotion, usually extending over days rather than hours, that colors a person's psychological life. A depressed child usually displays a depressed mood, although boredom, anger, or irritability can also signal depression.

Marcia, for example, complains of being bored, even in history class, which she used to love, and acts grouchy for no apparent reason. The 12-year-old frequently gets angry with her friends, which puts them off.

Loss of Pleasure

Tim, 10, formerly the life of the classroom, seems to have lost his capacity for fun. He passes up opportunities to play at recess, and has even turned down invitations to visit after school. His old friends have simply given up asking him to play.

Apathy toward activities a child formerly enjoyed commonly signals depression. Loss of interest can range from just not caring anymore—one boy said he still went out with his friends on Friday nights but that he was just going along out of habit—to a painful inability to experience any pleasure at all.

Low Self-Esteem

A depressed child views herself in a consistently negative light. When I asked her to describe herself, Peggy said she was "dumb." Other depressed children may say they are lazy, clumsy, or ugly. Peggy felt her family and teachers were disappointed in her and that she had let them down. Her constant refrain was "I can't do anything right."

Low self-esteem can become a self-fulfilling prophecy. The worse a child feels about herself, the more depressed she becomes. She tries fewer things and gives up more easily. Without perseverance, she'll fail more often and confirm her own low view of herself.

Feelings of Guilt

The depressed child may or may not say he feels guilty. But he may deliberately misbehave in school in order to be punished, or punish himself by destroying a favorite possession or by having many "accidents."

Nat, 13, says he has done many bad things, that he thinks bad thoughts, that he is mean to other students, and that when things go wrong, it's his fault. A depressed child may blame himself for things like getting a friend in trouble at recess, wasting the teacher's time, or letting down his teammates.

Pathological guilt accompanies depression in children just as it does in adults. Children may feel guilty about minor misdeeds or believe they have committed grave sins.

Social Withdrawal

Because depression reduces a child's interest in other people, social withdrawal commonly signals depression in children and adolescents.

Depressed children frequently have trouble making new friends and keeping their old ones. They may complain of feeling left out. In fact, research shows they actually do get teased more often than nondepressed children. Some depressed children openly reject their friends, while others set themselves up to be rejected, confirming their worthlessness in their own eyes.

Pam, for example, turns down invitations from friends and has stopped going out. At times, the 14-year-old is deliberately rude to her classmates. Unlike some other childhood emotional disturbances in which a child has never been able to form stable relationships, a depressed child has usually had normal friendships in the past.

Loss of Energy

A depressed child sits slumped in his chair or draped over his desk, and moves very little. He may answer questions with a word or two, in a monotone. Your child may ask to be excused from gym, complaining of stomachaches, headaches, or other maladies for which no medical explanation can be found.

At recess, Adam, 6, quits games early from fatigue or says he's too tired to play at all. He looks sluggish, and talks and moves slowly. He's having trouble falling asleep at night, so of course he tires easily during the day.

Trouble Concentrating

Lynn, 16, can't seem to concentrate in school. She complains of forgetting what she learns. She turns in incomplete assignments and fails to finish tasks that used to be easy for her. This deterioration in her school performance began quite suddenly.

Thoughts of Death

For weeks, Tony, 11, was so preoccupied with the death of his grandmother that he wrote about it in every composition. Depressed children may also express suicidal thoughts in their writings or drawings.

Cathy, 15, told her favorite teacher that she'd had dreams in which she was absent. "I have dreams about the years to come, and I see my family as I imagine they will be. But I am never there. I'm always absent, and no one seems to miss me."

Behavior Change

Depression can make a child's behavior change suddenly. Your normally calm child may become agitated and unable to sit still in class for more than a few minutes. Rapidly shifting from one activity to another, he appears to be searching fruitlessly for satisfaction.

Particularly in boys, depression frequently manifests itself as aggressive behavior. Jay, 9, was so belligerent in class, his teacher referred him to me. Jay constantly argued with his teachers and physically attacked his peers. He got into serious disciplinary trouble before his depression was recognized and treated.

Depression may also inhibit your child's behavior. He may become a passive observer of school activities and act submissive to his peers. Amy, 12, simply sits at her desk as if she were frozen. She said, "I don't even move in my sleep anymore. I wake up in the morning stiff, lying just the way I was the night before."

Hopelessness

James, 15, wrote several English compositions in which he predicted his early death. The conviction that things will never get better may be the most ominous feature of depression. Hopelessness destroys the motivation to change or to even to survive.

Hearing Voices

Some children describe hearing voices, inside their head or out, when no one else is around. Brittany, 10, told her teacher that she heard a chorus of voices telling her, "You're no good, you're a failure, and nobody likes you."

Auditory hallucinations may be a symptom of several mental disorders, including schizophrenia, drug intoxication, an organic mental disorder, or depression. Some studies suggest that depressed children are especially prone to hearing voices.

Anxiety

Anxiety often accompanies depression, ranging from assorted vague worries about the future to paralyzing delusional fears. Luke, 7, refused go out for recess for fear that an airliner would fall from the sky and kill him.

Themes of loss, abandonment, punishment, or harm frequently come up in the play and writing of depressed children. Chloe, 13, wrote a story in which her parents put her out to sea in a small boat where she drifted forever, crying in the darkness.

SIGNS YOU MIGHT SEE AT HOME

Your child may tell you she's having a hard time paying attention or keeping her mind on schoolwork. She may say she has no interest in school or finds it too hard, too boring, or "dumb." Perhaps, like Peggy, she's failing to complete her class assignments or homework.

Does your child complain of forgetting what she learned, or find new material impossible to master? If depression is causing her to lose sleep or appetite, she's bound to have trouble thinking and learning properly.

A depressed child may be very critical of herself, complaining, "I can't do anything right," or "I'm the worst player on the team and the worst student in the class." Or she may express feelings of loneliness: "I wish I had more friends, but nobody wants to play with me."

Your depressed child may become reluctant to go to school, saying things like, "I don't like school and I don't want to go," "I'm always tired at school," "School's too hard," or "Nobody likes me."

Or he may simply refuse to go to school. Max, a bright 11-year-old, began complaining of stomachaches shortly after his family moved to a new neighborhood and he had to change schools in the middle of the sixth grade. His doctor could find no physical cause for the stomachaches that were severe enough to keep Max home from school several days out of every week. Soon the boy was in danger of failing sixth grade.

Research reveals that children who refuse to go to school are likely to be depressed. Like the chicken and the egg, it's impossible to say whether depression causes absenteeism or whether prolonged absenteeism causes depression. Without intervention, though, the cycle will simply escalate. As a child like Max begins to fail, he'll become more hesitant to go to school and this will make him even more depressed.

HOW YOUR CHILD'S
SCHOOL CAN HELP

Our increasingly mobile society has deprived children of the stability that used to be part of living in a neighborhood where everyone knew each other. This old-fashioned neighborhood offered children a variety of emotional resources. There, if your mother wasn't home when you returned from school, you could always get your cookies and milk from the mother next door. Today, as families move more frequently, some people never set roots in a particular neighborhood. Increasingly, too, children are growing up in single-parent homes, dual-career homes, or in "blended" families. For children who lack traditional sources of stability—neighborhood and family—school may be a lone island of consistency in a sea of change. This fact makes it crucial to include school personnel in the therapeutic plan for a depressed child.

Jimmy's case offers a good example. By the time he was 12, Jimmy had lived in four different houses in three different neighborhoods. His mother had divorced and remarried three times. Jimmy's "family" has at various times included one father, two stepfathers, two brothers, two sisters, three stepbrothers, four stepsisters, as well as a niece and two nephews.

Realizing that Jimmy's school gave him his only stability, Jimmy's mother purposely remained in the same school district. But when Jimmy was in the sixth grade, one of his favorite teachers left in the middle of a term. Jimmy became seriously depressed.

When Jimmy's counselor called me in for a consultation about his behavior, I set out to include the school staff in Jimmy's therapy. Indeed, in many ways, the school personnel *were* Jimmy's family.

Of course, no one could bring Jimmy's teacher back. But once the school administrators realized how important school was in Jimmy's life, they fostered his relationships with two other key people: the school nurse and the counselor. Unlike teachers who teach a different group of children every year, the nurse and the counselor could be there for Jimmy until he graduated.

Jimmy's school nurse made it a point to get to school early so the boy could drop in to greet her. She also made herself available to soothe the inevitable hurts of Jimmy's daily life at school. Like the nurse, the counselor also made a special effort to be accessible. When Jimmy came to her with his problems, the counselor listened, comforted, and advised the boy. Both the nurse and the counselor helped

Jimmy emerge from his depression. For her part, Jimmy's mother stayed in touch with the school staff, and encouraged Jimmy's relationships with both the counselor and the school nurse.

Helping Your Child's Teacher Help Your Child

Like Jimmy's nurse and counselor, the staff at your child's school can help your depressed child simply by being there, day after day. You may also want to ask a particular staff person to make a special effort on behalf of your child, such as being on hand for daily visits.

Remember the theory, discussed in Chapter 3, that depression is a kind of learned helplessness. Because they are learning experts, your child's teachers may be able to offer a special kind of help to your depressed child.

For example, a skilled, informed teacher can help your child learn that bad events often have external causes and can encourage him to explore realistically what some of these might be. Your child's teacher can also help him recognize that things change, problems get resolved, and that even his personal characteristics can be changed with effort. Finally, your child can be helped to learn that though he is imperfect in some situations, he isn't flawed in every circumstance. The following examples demonstrate the many kinds of help both a skilled teacher and a sensitive parent can offer a depressed child.

Maximizing Success

Peggy felt stupid because she made so many mistakes in reading. Each school day, she faced the frustration and shame of stumbling over words and struggling with sentences.

Mrs. O'Connor recognized the impact of Peggy's reading difficulty on her mood and self-esteem. So she took the time to create opportunities for Peggy to read successfully, starting with simple books about dancers and ballet, a special interest of Peggy's. Mrs. O'Connor helped Peggy practice reading privately so that the girl would be able to get up and read before the class.

When her class responded to her knowledge about ballet, asking questions and paying attention to her answers, Peggy gradually began to feel more competent. Soon she was beginning to take the risk of reading even new material aloud. And she began to enjoy school and life again.

Minimizing the Negative

A sensitive teacher or parent can also help a child become aware of his negative thoughts. At 9, Jeremy's constant refrain was "I'm not good at anything; no one likes me. I never do anything right." His teacher helped Jeremy see how these thoughts were preventing him from doing things he *did* know how to do. Recognizing and labeling his negative thoughts began to give Jeremy a new level of control over them.

In order to help your depressed child, however, you first need to be sensitive to his feelings. If he maintains that he can't concentrate, insisting that he *can* will simply make your child feel contradicted when he's already feeling despondent. Acknowledge his feeling first: "It must be frustrating (or upsetting, or maddening) to feel you can't concentrate."

Afterward, try following up with some positive suggestions based on your own observations. For example, you might say, "I know it's hard and I know you're under a lot of pressure. But, even so, I've seen signs that you're able to do something. Why don't we see what you can do with a little peace and quiet and with a little help from me? Let's get your book and see how much of this page you can do." Dividing a task into manageable portions allows for graded successes.

Emphasizing the Positive

Remind your child that he frequently gets positive feedback about himself, and not just negative. Bill, 9, always focused on the negative and screened out any compliments he received from his teacher. The boy could always find evidence to confirm his negative view of himself. Bill's teacher made sure he also heard positive feedback and recognized the things he did well.

Taking a New Point of View

You can also help your child find alternative solutions to problems. Brainstorming alternative solutions comes most profitably at the end of several other steps in problem-solving. Take Melissa's case, for example. Melissa, a high school freshman, was frustrated because her mother didn't want her to try out for the soccer team. The girl dissolved into tears of frustration, crying, "I can't do anything, my parents never let me do anything, and I probably wouldn't make the team anyway because I'm no good."

First, Melissa needed help in labeling her feelings: fear, frustration, depression, and anger at her parents. Second, she needed to learn how to identify her goals: to make the soccer club, to get exercise, to improve her athletic skills, and to make some new friends. Third, Melissa needed to identify the obstacles that were preventing her from achieving her goals.

Melissa's approach to her parents was one of her biggest obstacles. Many depressed children can't say clearly what they want. They undermine their own goals either by not expressing their needs clearly or by being ambivalent or provocative.

Melissa needed help learning to say, "Mom and Dad, I'd like to be able to try out for the soccer club because I think it would be good exercise and I'd make new friends." Of course, she also needed to learn how to listen to her parents' concerns, whether they had to do with cost, transportation, or how the activity would affect her grades.

Once she heard their concerns, Melissa brainstormed with her parents about possible solutions—things such as finding a carpool, committing herself to spending an hour on homework before soccer, or getting one of her parents to help her learn to kick and dribble the ball. As a side benefit of this kind of brainstorming, Melissa improved her relationship with her parents.

Getting Specific

You can help your child be specific rather than vague about his concerns. When Justin cried, "I can't stand to be in school anymore!" his fifth-grade teacher questioned him gently and empathetically. Approached this way, Justin made the following realization: "I get very nervous when I think about taking a math quiz." This more specific problem lent itself to correction as he worked with his teacher on relaxation, on verbalizing fears about the quiz, and on improving his study skills.

Imagining Success

Try to help your child imagine going through the steps of a task and successfully completing it. Jennifer didn't know how she would even begin to do the eighth-grade report on China. Her social studies teacher guided her through the various steps and helped her imagine how successful she would feel when she was done.

Playing a Role

Your child can rehearse new social skills and new, more functional behaviors by role playing. In Mr. Soloway's fourth-grade class, for example, the children take turns role-playing healthy ways of dealing with stress and negotiating conflict.

Taking One Step at a Time

Work with your child to help fight her fear of failure. When Sarah refused to attempt things for fear of making mistakes, her seventh-grade teacher pointed out that doing an assignment only partially was much more useful than not doing it at all. She helped Sarah see that mistakes were just an indication of the things she still needed to learn.

Relinquishing Blame

Encourage your child to avoid personalizing every incident of bad luck. When it rained on the day of the fifth-grade field trip to the zoo, Mike acted as though it was a personal punishment meant for him. Without belittling Mike's feelings, his teacher told him, "It's just a bad break." As Mike progressed in his therapy, he became able to accept such bad breaks as occasional happenings that weren't his fault.

DEPRESSION AND LEARNING DISABILITY

Parent advocate groups increasingly favor the term "learning difference" to replace the term "disability." These

SIGNS OF A
LEARNING DISABILITY

- Difficulty understanding and following directions
- Trouble remembering what was just said
- Failure in basic math, reading, and writing skills
- Left-right reversals, letter reversals (b and d), number reversals (27 and 72), and word reversals (top and pot).
- Coordination difficulties, both gross motor (skipping, running, sports) and fine motor (writing, using scissors, tying shoelaces)
- Frequent forgetting or misplacing of materials or schoolwork
- Difficulty understanding time concepts

learning differences specifically involve difficulty listening, speaking, remembering, reading, writing, reasoning, or problem-solving in a child with otherwise normal intelligence. Learning-disabled children have no severe physically impediment such as impaired vision or hearing or mental retardation.

Unlike the child with a learning disability who has always had difficulty with certain learning tasks, a depressed child shows a sudden change in academic performance—a change that dates from the onset of the depression. And unlike a learning-disabled child, a depressed child may show considerable variance in performance from day to day or even from hour to hour, depending on her mood.

But your depressed child may be learning-disabled, too. If you suspect your child's depression stems from a learning disability, you might be right. Many children with learning differences also suffer from depression. In fact, one study of children at a special school for learning disabilities showed that the vast majority of these learning-disabled children were also depressed.

ADVOCATING FOR YOUR
CHILD IN SCHOOL

- U.S. Public Law 94-142 guarantees the right to an appropriate education and related services for children with a variety of handicaps including serious emotional disturbance.
- Your child has the right to an evaluation which may include educational, psychological, psychiatric, and neurologic components.
- Each student who qualifies must be provided an individualized educational plan (IEP), developed by the multidisciplinary evaluation team.
- If he requires them, your child is entitled to speech, language, occupational, or physical therapies, special educational modalities or placements, or other related services.
- As a parent, your due-process rights are guaranteed, and you are entitled to an impartial hearing regarding any part of the educational evaluation or plan.

Joanne, for example, has always hated school. Diagnosed as learning-disabled in the third grade, the 12-year-old defines herself as "dumb." It's not difficult to understand why poor self-esteem so often accompanies a learning disability. Struggling with basic tasks, failing repeatedly, and comparing unfavorably with peers—all these experiences differentiate the learning-disabled child from her classmates. She may feel inferior, stupid, slow, or incompetent at school. She may also be at a social disadvantage because of difficulty reading social cues or understanding the nuances of language.

If your child's school problems preceded her depression, have her assessed for a learning disability. This assessment can be obtained through the school at no additional cost at a parent's request (see box). The testing takes between four and eight hours, depending on the level of impairment and what disabilities are discovered in the process of testing.

Testing will evaluate your child's performance in the following areas: academic achievement; thinking style; ability to maintain attention and concentrate; ability to learn by looking and listening; capacity to store information for the short and the long term; ability to recall, integrate, sequence, and coordinate new learning; skill at speaking and writing; gross motor and fine motor control. The evaluation also includes a medical and psychological review to explore any conditions that may be contributing to your child's learning disability.

After this assessment, a group of concerned people will meet to develop a special plan for your child's learning needs. You and your child will meet with teachers and other school personnel, as well as outside psychologists or psychiatrists. Together, you will plan the approach that best serves your child's learning needs. If your child's disability is accompanied by a medical or biological disorder, a psychiatrist may also prescribe medication.

Helping Your Learning Disabled Child

Your depressed learning-disabled child needs considerable help accepting his disability for what it is—a specific variation in brain circuitry. Special—at times, extraordinary—compensatory efforts must be made for your child to keep up with the standard curriculum.

To help your child cope with his learning differences, adapt to the school environment, and develop alternative methods of learning, everyone must agree to understand the child in a similar way. Parents and teachers must coordinate their efforts to support the child's strengths and help him compensate for his weaknesses.

Bart, 12, has both a behavior disorder and a learning disability. His school called me because Bart had nearly stopped doing any work, even in his special-education classroom. Instead, he would just sit in school and stare off into space.

We held a meeting that included Bart, his mother, his teacher, the school social worker, and a psychiatrist. Before this meeting, Bart's mother and teacher had been embroiled in a long-standing conflict, each accusing the other of sabotaging Bart's education. That was because each saw Bart's problem and the solution differently. Bart's mother believed he should be allowed to use a typewriter in school, but Bart's teacher feared the machine might distract her other students. This struggle only exacerbated the boy's school problems.

At the meeting, Bart talked quite openly about how he saw his own problems in the classroom. He said he learns only by listening. When he tries to take any notes, he becomes confused and frustrated, so he gives up. He also spoke about how laborious it was for him to write. These problems stem from Bart's learning differences.

The group brainstormed and agreed on a plan whereby Bart could tape class discussions and do his written homework with a computer. Just a few weeks later, Bart's mother called to express her delight over the marked improvement in her child's mood and his schoolwork. Bart's teacher, too, commented on how much the boy's attitude had improved now that he was experiencing some success in school.

Sensitive teachers and parents should also look to create opportunities for success in areas unaffected by the child's learning disability—art, music, or dance, for example. A child's strengths and special talents can sometimes even be used to help him learn, just as Mrs. O'Connor used Peggy's interest in dance to help her learn to read.

Help your child break down large assignments into small, achievable goals, so that he can experience some success in school every day. Your child may find it easier to get his work done if he has an incentive to work toward. In Bart's case, for example, the group decided that for every set of finished assignments, Bart would earn a bowling trip with his mother. This was a great incentive because it was something they enjoyed doing together. Not only that— Bart could always beat his mother at bowling!

A FINAL WORD

Just because your child is depressed doesn't mean her school life can or should be put on hold. As much as possible, encourage your child to keep up with assignments and take part in extracurricular activities. Even if school-work frustrates your child, these activities can offer an important alternative avenue to self-esteem.

5

CHILDHOOD DEPRESSION AND BEHAVIOR PROBLEMS

—

Brian was referred to me by the local police for treatment. Not quite 13, he had already violated the law several times. On one occasion, Brian and a group of other children had broken into an unused summer home and destroyed some furniture. Another time, he and his friends had started a gasoline fire that burned down a shed and jeopardized nearby homes. Brian ignored his curfew repeatedly and had been suspended from school twice in the past month. His parents couldn't control him, and he didn't seem to want to control himself. The police saw Brian as just another delinquent headed for bigger trouble.

Severe behavior problems such as these may understandably prompt a parent, a teacher, or even the police or courts to seek psychiatric help for the child. Assessment frequently uncovers an underlying depression. Indeed, Brian suffered from both depression and a conduct disorder.

A child with a conduct disorder repeatedly does things that violate the rights of others as well as the rules of his family and society at large. A psychiatric diagnosis of conduct disorder means a child or teen manifests a pattern of misbehavior lasting at least six months and including acts such as stealing, running away, lying, fire setting, truancy, vandalism, cruelty to animals or people, fighting, or forcing someone into sex.

Unlike most children with a pure conduct disorder, however, Brian was troubled by his situation. He felt guilty about the damage he had done, and although he didn't like who he was becoming, he didn't know how to change. "At the time it's happening, when I'm doing something wrong, I don't think ahead. I'm with my friends, and somebody gets an idea, and it seems like it will be fun, sort of exciting. Later on I can see how it was stupid, but then it's too late."

Brian sounded like the boy in the aphorism "In his heart, every boy would rather steal second base than steal a car." But Brian was caught up in a pattern of loneliness and isolation. He didn't feel as if he belonged in the "right" group, with the boys who were successful athletes or students. Convinced he was a failure, Brian gravitated to the only kids he thought would accept him. He felt good only during the brief moments of "excitement" that got him into trouble.

Like Brian, about one-third of depressed children also show conduct disturbances. Not surprisingly, most parents notice the behavior problems first and learn about the depression only after their child is in therapy. In fact, many depressed children receive treatment only after their behavior has hoisted a red flag alerting their parents and teachers.

A child can engage in disturbing behavior without showing all the signs of a conduct disorder, however. Oppositional defiant disorder, a less severe behavioral disorder typically seen in younger children, involves behaviors such as temper tantrums, arguing with adults, defying or refusing adult requests, deliberately annoying or blaming others, using obscene language, irritability, resentfulness, and vindictiveness.

Often depression precedes such behavioral problems. In most of these cases, treating the depression usually makes the behavior problems disappear. But managing children who are both depressed and behaviorally disturbed poses a unique challenge to therapists. Because they have a greater tendency to act on their depressed feelings, these impulsive children and teenagers must be considered to be at high risk for suicide (see Chapter 7).

Researchers don't know what causes depressed children to develop conduct disorders. But one study revealed that compared to less aggressive boys, highly aggressive boys seemed to perceive others as hostile adversaries, failed to come up with effective solutions to problems, and could not anticipate the logical consequences of their aggressiveness. In short, these boys appeared to lack the ability to appreciate another person's point of view.

While many delinquent children come from loving homes, families of these youths do seem to suffer more than their share of parental mental illness or alcoholism, conflict, and stress. Many delinquent children report early peer group rejection, lack of adult supervision, culturally sanctioned aggression, and a general lack of respect for parents and authorities.

Depressed children of both sexes may well turn to drugs to "self-medicate" their depression (see Chapter 6). But while boys are more likely to act out in aggressive or destructive ways, depressed girls may be more likely to manifest sexually promiscuous behavior or to develop eating disorders.

For example, Lauren, 16, tried to kill herself after the most recent in a long string of boyfriends broke up with her. Lauren had a reputation as an easy mark at her high school. In therapy, she acknowledged that a lot of boys were attracted to her, but the pretty teenager claimed that she wasn't really easy and that it took "a lot" for her to have sex with someone. At the same time, she wondered whether the boys who said the right words and treated her well may just have been "smoother" than the others.

A bright girl, Lauren is failing most of her classes. She used to do well in school, but as it began to take more effort to succeed, she became frustrated and turned away from her studies. Lauren found it easier to win approval for her good looks, and she liked the increasing attention she got from the boys as she matured. But because she lacked a solid foundation of self-esteem, the girl depended completely on approval from others. Time and again, especially when her confidence was shaky, Lauren traded sex for the acceptance she desperately needed, even if it didn't last.

EATING DISORDERS

As many as four out of five patients with an eating disorder will also suffer depression at some point during their lives. In addition, many have relatives who report a history of depression.

Although eating disorders typically appear in adolescence, younger children may also develop these conditions. In fact, when researchers surveyed young children in grades three through six about weight preoccupation and dieting, they found that 45 percent of the children wanted to be thinner, 39 percent had tried to lose weight, and almost 7 percent were already at high risk for an eating disorder.

Studies of 9- and 10-year-old girls also reveal unhealthy patterns of dieting alternating with overeating. In fact, worries about being too fat may begin as early as kindergarten.

Eating disorders afflict about 8 million people in the United States, according to statistics from the National

Association of Anorexia Nervosa and Associated Disorders (see Resources). Females outnumber males by seven to one, but teenage boys may occasionally develop eating disorders in order to meet a weight qualification for a sport.

Anorexia Nervosa

Young people with anorexia share an unhealthy thinness, an intense preoccupation with food, a morbid fear of getting fat, a disturbed body image (feeling fat even though emaciated), and the cessation of normal menstrual periods. Anorexics typically experience depression during starvation, but they may remain depressed even after their weight normalizes. Their endocrine systems reveal the same disruptions as those of depressives.

Alicia came into the hospital because she was feeling suicidal. The 17-year-old anorexic announced, "If this is the life I've got, I don't want it."

"How would you want your life to be?" I asked.

Alicia answered, "I'd like to be thin, and popular with boys, and I don't want to fight with my mother anymore. That would make me very happy, but it will never happen."

"Why not?"

"Because my mother hates me; she hates the sight of me. And I've always been fat, no matter how little I eat, and no boy has ever been attracted to me."

That night Alicia had a dream: "I was rushing around trying to find a prom dress, but I couldn't find one to fit. They were all too small, too tight because I was so fat. I couldn't find one at any store, and it was the day of the prom. I finally found a dress, but then I had to find someone to go with, and I couldn't. No boy would go with me. I felt ugly and hurt and lonely, and then I woke up."

Alicia says that she doesn't remember anything before she was 12 when her father left home and divorced her mother. But she does remember this: "I was a super-happy child—that's what my mother says. I never cried and I laughed about everything. Of course, now I'm paying for it, like everything has to even out in your life. For being ecstatic then, I have to be drab now."

Bulimia Nervosa

This condition entails repeated episodes of binge eating, involving the rapid consumption of large amounts of food in a short period of time. Bulimic patients report a loss of control during binging, followed by self-induced vomiting, diuretic or laxative abuse, or compulsive exercising to prevent weight gain. Indeed, a preoccupation with body shape and weight takes over the bulimic's life, with many patients reporting that they think about food, weight, and body shape during most of their waking hours. In addition, bulimics suffer from low self-esteem, an overconcern with the opinion of others, difficulty expressing negative feelings, and problems regulating their own behaviors.

The media's—indeed the entire culture's—emphasis on thinness and dieting has made bulimia common among adolescents. These young people frequently come from upwardly mobile families, and they may have taken on their parents' traits of competitiveness, achievement orientation, and perfectionism. Their mothers may also be excessively concerned about their own weight and appearance.

Bulimics, like depressed youths who use drugs for self-medication, typically ingest massive doses of food in an attempt to soothe themselves or to cope with stress. For example, Doreen, 16, had been bulimic for the past three years and was in the hospital recovering from her most recent suicide attempt. When I met her, the girl lay in bed with an IV in her arm and a suction tube in her nose.

"I hate myself. I shouldn't be alive," Doreen cried.

"Why?"

"Because I just make trouble for everybody I love. Debbie was my last chance, the only one left who would keep me. Now she doesn't want me with her either."

Debbie was Doreen's stepmother's sister, who had taken the girl in six months ago after Doreen's father kicked her out. Doreen's father in turn had taken Doreen in when her mother had wanted to get rid of her three years earlier.

"Debbie found out that I'm bulimic," Doreen explained. "She found doughnut boxes and empty potato chip bags under my bed. She also found the big spoon in my bathroom that I use to make myself vomit. She asked me if I had started again and I had to admit that I had."

Hospitalized three years before, Doreen had temporarily overcome her bulimic symptoms with the help of behavioral treatment. But the girl's depression had never been adequately addressed in her earlier hospitalization.

"I just don't like myself; I never have," Doreen continued. "I've always hated the way I look and I've never felt like I deserved anything good. I've tried to talk about these feelings with my parents, but they don't believe me. They tell me that I'm lying, especially my dad. He yells at me and tells me that I'm making these things up to get attention just so someone would talk to me. I wasn't making up the bulimia, but I did want someone to talk to me."

WHAT YOU CAN DO

Because behavioral problems such as delinquency, sexual promiscuity, and eating disorders so frequently mask an underlying depression, be sure to ask the therapist to check for depression when you seek professional help for your child (see Chapter 9).

Antisocial or self-destructive behaviors can place your child at serious risk for continuing psychiatric disability, so you'll want to watch for behavior problems in your depressed child, and try to prevent or minimize them. Whether or not your depressed child currently displays behavioral problems, it certainly pays to know how to bring out your children's best behavior.

As the old song puts it, you need to accentuate the positive and eliminate the negative. In addition, it helps to be clear and consistent, to be realistic, and to seek the support of other parents or professionals.

Accentuate the Positive

Since most children can't obey and disobey at the same time, let yours know what you want them to do. For example, it's almost impossible to practice the piano and tease a younger sister simultaneously, so you might suggest that your child who is teasing his younger sister practice the piano now.

Of course, your child may begin teasing his sister after he practices the piano. That's why you need to come up with something he can do next and praise him for it afterward.

Expect the best from yourself and from your children. If you anticipate disappointment and failure, your children will probably "live down" to your expectations, but if you expect sincere effort and realistic success, you'll probably get them. Whenever possible, catch your child doing something right so you can acknowledge it and praise him.

You always want to build on your child's strengths. To do this, try to identify the things your child does well, concentrate on improvement rather than perfection, and give plenty of positive feedback along the way. But make sure your child knows you also value him for who he is apart from what he does or doesn't do. Everyone needs some unconditional positive regard for the proper development of self-esteem.

You can even look for a positive opportunity in a problem situation. For example, Christine had had a bad spring semester. In and out of the psychiatric hospital, the deeply depressed 15-year-old barely passed most of her courses. But she didn't make the cutoff in French. Now Christine faced repeating French I in the fall while all her friends progressed to French II. But then her mother got an idea.

Christine's mother was a part-time librarian at the town library, and she knew they needed some students for summer help. So she and Christine made a plan and set some goals for themselves. Christine would work 20 hours a week at the library, staying after an extra hour and a half each day to study French and listen to French tapes. Her mother would take some extra hours during June and July, and by August they would have saved enough money for a trip to France together. This plan turned into a mother-daughter adventure that the pair would never forget. It also proved to be just the right motivation for Christine, who made special arrangements to retake her final exam in the fall.

Every night before your child goes to sleep, take a few minutes to snuggle. Talk to your child about her day and about the good things that happened. You can even make a ritual out of sharing "one good thing that happened to me today." Build your child's positive self-image by discussing something you like about yourself and asking your child what she likes about herself. Then look forward to the next day by discussing something you each plan to do tomorrow. As you celebrate the positive elements of each day, you'll be getting in touch with your child in a very special way.

Try to avoid excessive pressure to succeed and let your child know that striving is more important than winning. Encourage your child's uniqueness, avoid comparisons with siblings or other children, actively solicit your child's opinion and help, and promote your child's self-reliance by never doing things for her that she can do for herself.

Parenting *is* a profession, so be professional. Keep calm, maintain your dignity, and work to control your anger and other impulsive, immature, or destructive behaviors. Your attitude toward your child should communicate authority as well as warmth.

Since you are your child's most important teacher, pay attention to the way you model, explain, and practice the behaviors you want your child to learn. One of the most important skills you can demonstrate to your child is problem-solving. When you are frustrated about failing to accomplish a goal, you can act to change the situation, change your goal, or reduce the importance of the goal. Discuss your progress in this skill with your child.

Of course, you'll need to be patient. Behavioral change comes slowly, and parenting is hard work. Take time to think—about your child, his needs, his requests, and his behavior. Don't feel pressured to answer everything immediately or to solve every problem instantly. In fact, you want to show your children the importance of careful deliberation and patience. Give yourself credit for your efforts to be a good parent in the same way you're acknowledging your child's efforts.

Try to keep perspective, too. Behavior problems are common, but they are usually manageable. Ask yourself how your child's behavior compares in importance with other aspects of your current life. Try to assess just how significant his behavior is in the long run, compared with what has gone before and what is to come in your life.

As you probably know, any problem can expand to occupy your total attention. Your child's problem can spill over into every area of your life—your job, your marriage, your social life—and prevent you from enjoying anything. But don't let it. If you keep your child's behavior where it belongs, you'll be able to take better care of yourself. This includes eating right, getting some exercise you enjoy, nourishing your relationship with your partner, and building in sufficient time to relax.

Eliminate the Negative

Guilt over your parenting performance won't help your child any more than it will help you, so try to forgive yourself for the mistakes you've made in the past. Work to change what you're responsible for, and try to let go of what you're not.

Since punishment is the least effective way of changing behavior, use it sparingly. Never humiliate or ridicule your child. If he needs reminding when he's doing something wrong, make it short and simple, and take him aside to do it if he would be embarrassed otherwise.

Although you can ignore some minor infractions, jump in early when your child begins to engage in behavior that typically escalates into a major problem. Sweating the small stuff allows you to get control of your household before it's too late. As one seasoned child worker on the unit for delinquent adolescents used to say when he saw a certain looking-for-trouble expression on the kids' faces, "Don't even think about it, buster."

You can best extinguish negative, attention-seeking behavior by ignoring it. Respond to rebellious, power-seeking, or control-seeking behavior by staying out of the power struggle. Don't fight or give in, but rather, refuse to engage in the conflict. Work instead on negotiation and compromise, or perhaps save the discussion for a later time.

For example, Sam, 16, maintained that his mother was "cheap" because she refused to buy him a very expensive pair of jeans to cut down into shorts. As they left the store, he yelled, "I'm never going shopping with you again!" Sam's mother fought back her impulse to respond angrily, and said instead, "I'm sorry you feel that way, but I really want to buy you a pair of shorts today because it's going to be eighty-five degrees tomorrow. Why don't we try one more store and see if we can't find something that you like and that I think is worth the money." They bought a pair of shorts at the second store and came home still talking to each other, a major victory for both of them.

Instead of insulting your child with "you-messages"—"How can you be such a slob?" or "You're so careless about staying out past your curfew"—send "I-messages" that describe how you feel when your child does something. For example, you might say, "When you . . . (name the behavior or situation), I feel . . . (say specifically how you feel about the effect of the situation on you) . . . because . . . (state your reason). "I want . . . (say what you want done)." For example, Sam's mother told him, "When you stay out past your curfew, I get worried because the roads are dangerous. I want you to call by ten if you're going to be late."

Try to avoid problem-solving or negotiating when you're angry, tired, busy, or rushed. A single mother and her depressed adolescent son described their typical nightly struggle. Jim explained, "The problem is, I may do something she doesn't like, such as having friends in the house when she's not there, but then she goes ballistic. She completely loses it, yelling and screaming and embarrassing me in front of my friends."

Jim's mother acknowledged, "It's true. He's right; I do lose it. But that's because I'm stressed out. I don't get home from work until eight o'clock at night, and I've already taken everything I can take that day. When I find him sitting there eating pizza with a bunch of his friends, without my permission, without even asking me, I lose it. And I yell and scream.

"I don't like to lose control," Jim's mother continued. "I don't like the feeling and I'm mad at myself afterwards. It's not the kind of parent I want to be or even the kind of person I want to be."

Be Clear and Consistent

Every expert will tell you to be clear and consistent; you can read it in every single magazine article and book on disciplining children. That's because it's true and it works.

Younger children and even older children who have trouble controlling themselves seem to do best with a routine. They need to know what comes first, and what comes next. Keep your household schedule regular so that your children know, for example, that dinner comes every night at 6, that after dinner everybody has a job to do in cleaning the kitchen, and that nighttime is the time for doing homework or playing a family game.

For younger children, bath time may come at 7:30, and afterward you can plan on 10 or 15 minutes for a story, with lights out at 8. You may want to set a family rule about television watching for older children after they have finished their homework.

Since an optimal amount of frustration stimulates effort, mastery, and growth, show confidence in your child by not overprotecting her. Whenever it makes sense, solicit her opinion or advice, and be sure you give her age-appropriate responsibilities at which she can succeed.

Your biggest challenge as a parent is to grant your child increasingly more freedom within age-appropriate limits. This encourages your child to make choices and to accept the consequences of those choices. Older children need rules, but these should be focused on their increasing independence and not so unreasonable that they feel they must rebel against them.

For example, Jean, 15, was in the hospital because she had threatened to kill herself. She said, "My dad had grounded me for two years because I went with friends to a guy's house and stayed overnight. So they took everything away from me. My parents think I'm horrible, but I'm not. I don't do drugs, don't drink alcohol, and I'm not having sex. A 15-year-old like me is hard to find today.

"I'm good most of the time," Jean continued, "but if I screw up just once it becomes a major thing. They never say anything when I do good things like chores around the house, babysitting for my brothers while my mother works, or helping out on our new house. Actually, I'm a good student, I do my homework every night, I play on the soccer team, and I coach a soccer team. I'm in the drama club and the Spanish club. I take a lot of responsibilities and I'm good at them, but if I screw up just once I'm grounded for two years. I want my parents to stand back and let me grow up. They can set some reasonable rules. I don't mind rules; I need them. But I don't want them to take over my whole life. I don't mind advice, but I don't want to be controlled."

Try not to get down on yourself when you make mistakes or fail to deal with every single infraction as you had planned. You're not perfect, nor do you need to be. All you have to remember is the importance of consistency and to keep striving for it.

Being consistent in discipline is particularly important. In fact, the effectiveness of a consequence for misbehavior depends not on its severity but on how consistently it's applied. Predictability gives your child something she can count on. So you might say, "If you hit your brother, you'll get a time-out for fifteen minutes . . . the first time, every time. Bank on it, kiddo."

Keep discipline simple by setting reasonable goals. You can even choose one or two behaviors to work on at a time. If necessary, break behaviors down into manageable parts that your child can succeed at and you can reinforce. For example, if you want your 10-year-old to clean his room, a disaster area strewn with baseball cards, dirty T-shirts, and fruit flies hovering over an unidentified glob of organic material in the corner, overcome your instinct to declare, "Your room is a pigsty. I want every bit of it cleaned up and don't show your face out of this room until it's finished."

Your child will be better able to handle the job if you break it down into small steps. First, suggest he get all his dirty clothing into a basket in the hall. Second, all clean clothes, if there are any, should go into a closet or drawer.

Third, all books, magazines, and lost homework sheets get put into the bookcase. Fourth, decaying pizza, cookies, and wads of bubblegum go to the garbage.

Maintain clear rules and expectations. In some cases a written "code of conduct" is useful. You might try a behavior contract that sets out very clearly what behavior you expect of your child and what privileges he can hope to gain by behaving responsibly (see Resources).

By being clear and consistent, you provide your child with structure in the form of a schedule of times to do things and times not to do things, and an environment that has boundaries and limits, such as a bedroom for reading and sleeping, a dining room for eating in but not for throwing a ball, a backyard for playing ball in but not going beyond the fence. You must provide structure for your child and adolescent until she develops sufficient internal structure so that she can set limits for herself in a relatively unrestricted world.

Let your child know clearly what the consequences for misbehavior will be: If you choose to do that, then this will happen. Your actions will speak louder than your words. Indeed, the younger your child, the more his understanding and communication depend on actions rather than on words. Doing something as a consequence of your child's misbehavior will mean a lot more to your child than merely saying you are going to do it.

That's because consequences help to determine future behavior. Now consequences may be natural or logical. Burning your hands on a hot stove or freezing them if you don't wear mittens in winter represent natural consequences. Logical consequences are those that you apply, such as making your child walk to school if she misses the bus. Logical consequences should follow from a child's behavior, should be immediate, should be proportional, should be healthy, and should not be associated with anger or revenge. In fact, you can even involve your children in negotiating logical consequences.

Kelly, 8, was frequently late for school, for example, but a dangerous intersection made it unsafe to allow her to walk when she missed the bus. She and her mother agreed that when she missed the bus and had to be driven by her mother, Kelly would have to pay "cab fare" out of her allowance.

Be Realistic

Nobody's perfect; not only can you not be a perfect parent, your children will probably never be perfect either. Accepting yourself means becoming aware of your own strengths and weaknesses and striving to do better. Realize that every parent makes mistakes, and that you needn't think of them as catastrophic. Actually, mistakes can provide a powerful learning opportunity for both you and your child.

Once you recognize what you can and cannot control, begin to work on the things you can. For example, you can never regulate what your child thinks, feels, says, or does. Major power struggles between parents and children frequently arise around issues that the parent really cannot control and the child knows it—eating and sleeping, for example.

To some extent you can control simple things, especially with younger children, such as whether they are at home or at the park, in the family room or in their bedroom. But you can't make your child listen, and you can't force him to care about his work or about other people.

In fact, the only person you can control is yourself. But you *can* control what *you* say and do, what you will pay attention to and what you will ignore; what kind of communication you will respond to and what kind you won't; whom you will permit to use your telephone, television, your house for entertaining, or your car; and when and under what circumstances you'll allow these uses. You can also decide what the consequences will be for infractions.

Find Support

You may have particular problems dealing with your child's behavior if you suffer from depression yourself, if you have few sources of outside support, or if you are a single parent going it alone. But you don't need to raise your children in isolation. Instead, seek information from books like this one, and solicit advice and help from reliable relatives, friends with children, teachers, mental health professionals, and clergy.

Families today tend to be isolated, partly because of an extreme competitiveness about their children. Parents hesitate to admit that they struggle. They don't want to seek advice because they might look inadequate. But you don't need to be defensive about having behavior problems with your kids. Everybody has such problems.

In fact, when I'm talking with a group of parents about child behavior problems and I describe some of the problems I have with my own kids, the audience usually loves it. They're not happy that I have problems, but they're relieved that even a child psychiatrist has to struggle to figure out how to get his kids to behave.

So don't deal with your child's disturbed behavior in a vacuum. Talk over your concerns with your child and with other parents. Seek out "veteran" parents who have raised a few kids as well as parents who have children the same age as your child is now. And if you discover someone who approached the same problem differently and got better results, find out what worked for her and why.

6

CHILDHOOD DEPRESSION AND SUBSTANCE ABUSE

On the advice of both police and school officials, Mark's father took him to a drug counselor. Mark met with the counselor as often as three times a week, but the 16-year-old couldn't seem to stay away from cocaine for more than a few days at a time. Conceding failure, the counselor referred Mark to an intensive outpatient drug rehabilitation program for adolescents. There the boy spent four to five hours a day in 12-step groups, drug education programming, and individual and family counseling.

But Mark continued to use cocaine frequently. At the insistence of the rehab program director, Mark agreed to go into the hospital, where confinement in a locked unit finally broke his physical dependence on the drug.

Some kids bounce back quickly after coming off cocaine. Detoxified users frequently look healthier, sleep better, and regain their former energy level. But not Mark. The boy looked worse after he stopped using cocaine. Listless and withdrawn, Mark presented a stark contrast to the cocky, fast-talking character who had sauntered into the hospital.

That was because Mark's problem went beyond drug use. This teenager was deeply depressed. As it turned out, Mark had been medicating himself for several years with cocaine and assorted other substances. Most of the time, Mark used drugs not really to get high, but just to feel normal. Mark's drug counselors, with their tunnel vision trained on the chemical dependence issues, had completely missed the fact that the boy was self-medicating a depression.

Mark responded well to the same antidepressant medication that had worked for his depressed uncle, and he returned home in less than three weeks. In addition to a 12-step recovery program, Mark required psychiatric and medication follow-up. This combination treatment helped him conquer both his drug habit and his depression.

Like Mark, many adolescents come to psychiatric attention for an underlying depression only after being hospitalized for drug use. In fact, one study found that over 80 percent of teenagers entering an inpatient drug treatment facility also had a major psychiatric diagnosis. Alcohol abuse predominates among depressed adolescents, and it's not hard to understand why. Like adults, teenagers frequently self-medicate, that is, they use drugs like alcohol to alleviate distressing symptoms such as insomnia and anxiety.

Of course, doctors can't always tell whether an adolescent's drug use stems from depression or whether the drug use itself has produced depression, school failure, and troubled relationships. Since the abuse of many different drugs can result in symptoms that mimic depression, it's often impossible to know how much the drug effects are contributing to the depressive symptoms.

But it doesn't matter. If your depressed child is using alcohol or other drugs, his substance use must be treated whether it caused his depression or resulted from it. Substance use threatens your child's life. And his depression will never improve until his drug use is interrupted.

Even if your depressed child has shown no interest in drugs, you should become informed about drug use *before* it's a problem. In this chapter you'll find out how widespread drug use has become among young people; why so many teens use drugs; how you can tell if your child is involved in drugs; the major effects of commonly used drugs; and what you can do to help.

HOW COMMON IS DRUG USE?

If you're reading this chapter and thinking, "Not *my* kid," or "We don't have a drug problem in *our* community," think again. A survey in 1987 revealed that 58 percent of American high school seniors had tried illegal drugs at least once. Almost two out of three seniors admitted using alcohol in the month before the survey. One in five smoked cigarettes daily.

A more recent survey showed that 92 percent of American high school seniors drank alcohol occasionally or regularly, 54 percent smoked marijuana, 26 percent used stimulants, and 17 percent snorted cocaine.

Don't dismiss these statistics by recalling the cigarettes you furtively smoked in the bathroom or the beers you sneaked from your parents' refrigerator. Today's teens don't necessarily stop with a few cigarettes and a six-pack. Increasingly, adolescents are progressing to marijuana, LSD, cocaine, crack, uppers, downers, narcotics, inhalants, and a huge array of widely available designer drugs that are far more dangerous than anything you may have tried when you were young.

As you probably know, these drugs carry a variety of serious side effects, including memory loss and organ damage. Their use can lead to infections, high-risk sexual behavior under the influence, auto accidents while intoxicated, and school failure. Of course, the legal drug most teens find around the house—alcohol—is hardly innocuous either. Eight out of ten adolescent deaths occur by accidents, suicide, or homicide, and fully half of these deaths are alcohol-related.

Most teenagers will simply experiment with alcohol and other drugs, and the majority of these children will either stop using drugs or will remain casual users. While you needn't condone such behavior in your child, you should be aware that the majority of teens who use alcohol and other drugs experimentally do *not* go on to become regular users who psychologically depend on drugs or addicts who physically require them.

But a substantial minority of casual users do go on to use drugs regularly. Some of these children will become dependent, causing serious problems for themselves and others. Some will die in accidents, suicides, or overdose; and some will cause others to die.

Unfortunately, no simple method can predict which children will stop at experimentation and which will become psychologically or physically dependent on drugs. Therefore, you should consider any substance use by your child a serious matter.

I'm not talking just about teenagers here. Younger and younger children have begun to sample the drugs that are increasingly available in junior high schools and even in middle schools. Some chemically dependent youths have told me they first used drugs as early as age 9.

In a book called *Burnt* (New American Library, 1989), a young adult named Craig Fraser tells of his recovery from addiction to a mind-boggling variety of drugs. Fraser writes, "The first drug I ever experimented with was alcohol because it was so easy to get. I was in sixth grade and I wanted to know what it felt like to drink. One year later, I tried pot. That's the way it was with almost everyone I knew."

WHY DO CHILDREN USE DRUGS?

Like Craig Fraser, your child may experiment with alcohol, pot, or other drugs because they are so "easy to get" and because they make her feel good. The same way many adults like to have a drink to loosen up at a social gathering, children and teenagers often seek the disinhibiting effects of drugs. For a depressed child, drugs may alleviate uncomfortably sad feelings or allow her to escape a painful reality.

Children and teenagers may try drugs out of simple curiosity. Or they may use them to defy authority to do something they've been told not to. But in this case, actions truly speak louder than words. Teens are especially likely to use drugs if their parents or other family members do. Like adults, children and teenagers use drugs to relieve boredom, experience a thrill, or cope with stress.

The all-important peer group can put a lot of pressure on a teenager to try drugs. Drugs may be the only way your child feels he can make friends or be accepted by a particular group. And because adolescents tend to consider themselves indestructible, they often show little fear of the hazardous short- and long-term effects of drugs.

Our culture also promotes a child's acceptance of drugs. Watching just an hour's worth of commercials on television will convince even a jaded viewer that popping a pill can cure just about any problem at all. The glamorization of alcohol and tobacco in advertisements and attractive cartoon characters probably wields even greater influence over children than it does over adults. Recent research shows that some tobacco companies are specifically targeting children with such advertising.

HOW TO TELL IF YOUR CHILD HAS A DRUG PROBLEM

Because of the wide availability of drugs, parents of all teenagers should maintain a healthy level of suspicion about their children. And because depressed children are particularly likely to use drugs, parents of depressed teenagers should be even more vigilant.

Unfortunately, it's not always easy to tell if your child is using drugs. Since most teenagers don't see drug use as a problem, they may view you as a detective, trying to catch them and deprive them of something they want and feel entitled to. For that reason, many teenagers will lie if you ask them directly about their drug use. The information that you may have received from teachers, friends, siblings, and school personnel will frequently suggest that your teenager is much more seriously involved with drugs than your child will admit to.

But even when a child gives a fairly clear indication that he is using drugs, many parents persist in ignoring the signs. Why? Denial. Denial means avoiding the awareness that a real problem exists.

Sean, 17, began missing baseball practice frequently and finally quit the team. His parents figured he "just wasn't into the competitive thing" anymore, even though the boy had been a gifted athlete. Sean's grades dropped for two semesters in a row, but his parents attributed this to his paying more attention to his girlfriend than to his studies. When Sean was arrested for driving under the influence, his parents brushed it off because it was the homecoming dance, a "special occasion." When they found a marijuana pipe in the car one Sunday morning, Sean's parents let it go because Sean told them the pipe must have been left there by an acquaintance he had driven home. Now, five months later, Sean has a serious drug problem. He's been fired from two jobs, he probably will not graduate from high school this year, and he has lost all his friends outside the druggie crowd.

Parent Denial

It's a normal human tendency to want to avoid a painful situation. Many parents do this by denying that their child is using drugs or by refusing to face up to the extent of their child's problem. Ignoring your child's possible drug use may temporarily spare you the pain of awareness, but it can be life-threatening to your child.

Your child may have told you, for example, that his eyes are red from all that chlorine in the swimming pool. Or you may hear that your daughter has "no idea" where the marijuana cigarette in her room came from, or that she was simply "keeping a package for a friend."

You are engaging in denial if you simply accept stories like this at face value. Of course, you *want* to believe your child, because the truth threatens both your self-esteem and your concept of yourself as a good parent. But denying your child's problem may be the greatest obstacle to getting him the help he needs.

In fact, your denial ensures that your child's problem, whether it be drug or alcohol abuse or depression, will simply persist and worsen. Denial can protect your sense of complacency and your pride for only so long. When your child's drug problem becomes more severe—as it probably will—reality will eventually break through and overwhelm your denial.

Child Denial

Most likely, you're not the only one in your house who would prefer to deny your child's drug use. Your child, too, is probably also using denial to spare herself the pain of

WARNING SIGNS OF DRUG USE

The following symptoms should alert you to the fact that your child may be using drugs:

- Sudden changes in mood or behavior
- Loss of energy or fatigue
- Increase in physical complaints
- Red, bloodshot, or dull glazed eyes; use of eye drops
- Slurred speech or mental confusion
- Memory loss
- Loss of interest in activities such as sports
- Deteriorating schoolwork, falling grades
- School absences and disciplinary problems
- Conflict with or withdrawal from family
- Change in peer group, dress, or music
- Lying, denying, secretiveness
- Illegal behavior
- Drugs or drug paraphernalia turning up in your house or car

facing up to reality. To herself she may say, "I can handle it," or "I can stop any time I want," or "My drug problem isn't nearly as bad as my friend's." To you, your child will probably say whatever he thinks will get you off her case. But the sooner both of you face up to the facts, the sooner you can get the help you need.

Facing Up

If your child has shown one or more of the behaviors on the preceding list, you're probably a little scared and maybe more than a little angry. Try to keep calm, though, because you need to know more before you decide what to do.

First of all, find out whether your child's drug use is occasional or frequent. You should take even experimental or occasional use seriously, but you may block all communication if you treat your child like a drug addict after an isolated use.

Simply tell your child what you have discovered. Make it clear that any drug use is unacceptable to you and that you will be watching closely and monitoring future behavior. Then do it. While you can't follow your child everywhere, you can certainly apply sanctions that will make future drug-taking more difficult. Issue explicit rules about curfews, and about not associating with kids who use drugs. Explain that you will be watching for signs of drug use. Spell out the consequences for not following your rules, and make sure you carry them out.

If your child is using drugs more than experimentally, you should arrange to have her evaluated by a professional who has experience with adolescent substance abuse. A trained professional will probably be better able than you to determine just how serious your child's drug use is and to recommend appropriate treatment.

For example, a child who has dabbled in drugs may simply need to get some realistic education on the dangers of drugs. A child who uses drugs more regularly probably needs individual or group counseling in an outpatient setting. Outpatient therapy can work if an adolescent does not need detoxification, if he can successfully abstain from drugs during treatment, and if he is working or in school. Like Mark, a child who has become physically dependent on drugs may require temporary treatment in a hospital (see Chapter 10).

Screening

Analyzing a child's blood and/or urine for drugs can sometimes indicate that she has used particular drugs. Drug screening should be considered for adolescents with the following conditions:

1. New psychiatric symptoms such as hallucinations
2. High-risk behaviors like running away or delinquency
3. Sudden changes in mood, behavior, or mental
   functioning
4. Recurrent unexplained respiratory symptoms
5. Recurrent accidents or unexplained physical complaints

Teens with a history of drug use who are being monitored
for abstinence will probably also be screened.

Drug screens must be interpreted with care, however.
Decoding a drug screen requires a working knowledge of
drug kinetics, the time course of metabolism and clearance
from body tissues, as well as the sensitivities of various drug
assays. A negative screen does not prove that your adolescent
has not used drugs, nor does a positive screen mean that the
particular drug identified has caused all his symptoms.

For example, "designer drugs" are synthetic analogs or
mimics of federally controlled substances. Every bit as
dangerous as their models, these pretenders can neverthe-
less elude toxicology screening.

In addition, THC, the active element in marijuana,
lingers in the body for long periods, so significant amounts
will show up for many days after usage has stopped. In
fact, trace amounts of THC can still be detected after a
month or two of nonuse. Therefore, finding THC in the
urine of a patient who was admitted to treatment for
marijuana abuse one week ago does not necessarily mean
he has smoked marijuana since beginning treatment.

WHAT YOU NEED TO
KNOW ABOUT DRUGS

If you tried to make a list of the drugs children use to get
high, you'd probably just skim the surface. Everyone has

heard of alcohol, marijuana, cocaine, heroin. But did you know that some children get high on the gas in aerosol cans of whipped cream or paint? Or that the LSD that was so popular in the 1960s has made a comeback among junior high and high school students in an even stronger form?

Drug use frequently begins with legal and supposedly "less serious" drugs like tobacco and alcohol, and then usually progresses through a series of stages to illegal and "more serious" drugs. Most children and teenagers begin by using beer or wine. Then they smoke cigarettes and consume hard liquor. Marijuana usually comes next. Finally, teens seek out more dangerous drugs. Since advanced users often continue to use the "gateway" drugs (tobacco, alcohol, marijuana), multiple drug abuse or polydrug abuse has become a growing problem.

The effects of any drugs your child takes will depend on several factors: how he takes the drug; how large and pure the dose is; how frequently he uses it, and his expectations. For example, phencyclidine (PCP), an animal tranquilizer that is extremely popular among some adolescent groups, can produce stimulant, sedative, or hallucinogenic effects, depending on the dosage. In addition, many users combine different drugs, hoping to achieve many effects at once. Spacebase, for example, mixes PCP and crack cocaine.

For the sake of discussion, we can categorize drugs abused by adolescents into four main groups: stimulants, depressants, hallucinogens, and inhalants. We'll include marijuana, steroids, and narcotics in a group labeled "other."

Stimulants

These drugs, sometimes called uppers, activate a pleasure center in the brain. Stimulants include caffeine pills; amphetamines such as Benzedrine and Dexedrine; nicotine;

and cocaine. These drugs speed pulse rates and increase blood pressure, and they may contribute to insomnia and appetite suppression. Overdoses of stimulants can lead to hallucinations, convulsions, and possible death.

Since they contain nicotine, tobacco products like cigarettes and chewing tobacco must be considered drugs, too. Some parents breathe a sigh of mistaken relief to find that their children are "only" using tobacco, yet nicotine is highly addictive and of course tobacco is associated with numerous health hazards. Furthermore, recovering adolescents who begin to relapse frequently return to nicotine first.

Used as a powder, free base, or as the highly addictive crack, cocaine has recently become a serious problem among adolescents. Crack cocaine is a combination of cocaine hydrochloride and baking soda that, when smoked, enters the bloodstream directly from the lungs and delivers a quick, concentrated dose to the brain. The immediate euphoric rush coupled with its brief duration make crack a highly addicting agent with marked potential for compulsive use. Like crack, "ice" produces a dramatic rush, but the effects of this smokable form of methamphetamine last for hours instead of minutes.

Perhaps because of the drug's euphoric effects, depressed teenagers like Mark often favor cocaine. When used chronically, cocaine can trigger a particularly severe depression between intoxications.

Depressants

Depressants, or downers, slow the brain and central nervous system. Alcohol, barbiturates, and tranquilizers like Librium and Valium are all depressants. Overdoses of these drugs can lead to respiratory depression, coma, or death; and withdrawal poses serious medical risks of its own.

' Of course, alcohol, especially beer and wine coolers, remains the most commonly abused drug among adolescents. Alcohol is highly addictive, producing both physical and psychological dependence in abusers. Drinkers tend to develop tolerance, meaning that they require more and more alcohol in order to achieve the same level of intoxication. Chronic alcohol abuse can lead to many health complications, including liver and cardiac damage, gastritis, and peptic ulcer disease. Alcohol also contributes significantly to homicide, suicide, and traffic fatalities.

Alcohol produces intoxication at blood levels around 100mg/ml, and causes progressively greater physical impairments at higher levels or with sensitive individuals. A child who is using alcohol or inhalants will probably smell like whatever she is drinking or inhaling. In the case of barbiturates or tranquilizers, your child may appear drunk without any associated odor.

Hallucinogens

Drugs such as LSD, PCP, MDA, DMT, STP, mescaline, peyote, and psilocybin relax inhibitions and can cause hallucinations that affect a person's thinking, awareness, and sensations. Many hallucinogens soon become tolerated in larger and larger doses.

LSD can induce panic, suspiciousness, and feelings of helplessness in its users. Long after taking LSD, a user may experience flashbacks, in which he re-experiences the drug's effects without taking it again.

PCP, popularly known as angel dust, can spark uncontrollable fear and violent behavior. It has been responsible for suicides as well as homicides.

Inhalants

Because they cost little and can be obtained easily, inhalants have become the drug of choice for younger children.

Inhalants include gasoline, butane, toluene products (glues, acrylic paints, paint thinners), halogenated hydrocarbons (freon, solvents, spot removers, typewriter correction fluid), nitrous oxide (dental anesthetics, whipped cream propellants, automotive power boosters), and alkyl nitrites/nitrates, called poppers or snappers (room deodorants, liquid incense).

Inhalants can cause serious damage to the body's nervous system, as well as the brain, bone marrow, liver, and kidneys. They have been known to cause suffocation and sudden death as well.

Other

MARIJUANA   Of all the illegal abusable substances, marijuana remains the most popular. Hybrid forms of marijuana like sinsemilla ("seedless") contain much more of the active ingredient, tetrahydrocannabinol (THC), rendering it even more potent.

Commonly thought to be relatively harmless, this drug is actually extremely psychologically addictive. Furthermore, it impairs reflexes and reduces short-term memory, learning ability, and motivation. Marijuana can reduce testosterone levels, suppress sperm production, interfere with the female menstrual cycle, and compromise the body's immune system. And marijuana contains half again as many cancer-causing tars as tobacco. Since people who smoke marijuana usually try to hold it in their lungs for a prolonged period, smoke damage may be considerable. Finally, marijuana frequently opens the gate to further drug use.

ANABOLIC STEROIDS   Increasingly popular among teenagers, anabolic steroids (called 'roids, the juice, pump, or hype) build body muscle mass and enhance athletic performance. Some athletes start taking steroids because they think they must do so in order to win. Other teens use them to grow bigger and stronger at any cost. But steroids can cause mood swings, depression, and aggressive behavior. Physical effects include shrinking of testicles, sterility, acne, elevated blood pressure and blood cholesterol, and increased risk of heart disease and heart attacks. Abruptly stopping these drugs after prolonged use can cause depression or even suicide, so it's not surprising that some users continue taking them just to avoid feeling down. Considering these potential risks, steroids should be considered serious drugs of abuse even though they aren't used to get high.

NARCOTICS   The abuse of opiates has persisted for years. Injectable heroin has been perhaps the best known opiate to be abused, but people have also abused opium, morphine, methadone, codeine, Dilaudid, Percodan, and Darvon. Although adolescents use narcotics less commonly than the drugs discussed earlier, narcotics have extraordinary addictive potential. Parents must consider narcotics extremely dangerous. Withdrawal effects include stomach cramps, nausea, diarrhea, sweating, and chills. Overdose can produce respiratory depression and death.

WHAT YOU CAN DO

Since preventing a problem is always easier than solving it, prepare yourself by anticipating your child's interest in drugs. If you suspect your child already has a drug problem, don't hide behind denial. Acknowledge the problem and make a realistic plan of action. Of course, one of the most important things you can do is to set a good example yourself. Finally, you must follow through on your child's treatment plan.

Anticipating the Problem

To prevent your children from using drugs, get informed and provide realistic information for them. Take some books out of the library (see the References section), read them, and make yourself available to answer your children's questions.

You might also want to contact a parents' group, such as National Families in Action. This organization sponsors community programs on drugs and runs the National Drug Information Center, a clearinghouse of information on drug use (see Resources).

Not surprisingly, the children most vulnerable to peer pressure to use drugs share these characteristics: low self-esteem, a high need for acceptance by the group, and nothing else to do. Your child will be less likely to use drugs if he has a sense of direction in life and experiences good relationships with other people, including you. Encourage your child to develop interests that don't involve drugs or alcohol. Buy mountain bikes and learn to ride. Or take a scuba-diving class together at the YMCA. Through such activities, you'll be helping your child build self-esteem and conquer boredom.

Help your growing child to think of ways to say no and avoid peer pressure to drink or use drugs. Read *Peer Pressure Reversal* by Sharon Scott and do the exercises with your kids. Discuss these inevitable pressure situations with him in advance. You can help your child recognize and avoid situations where the likelihood for drug use is high. If someone tries to pressure your child to use drugs, you might suggest avoidance tactics such as the simple excuse, "It makes me sick."

Acknowledging the Problem

Since experimentation with drugs and alcohol is the rule rather than the exception for today's adolescents, prepare to set realistic limits. If your child's drug use goes beyond casual experimentation, learn where you can get help.

With respect to drugs and alcohol, I believe that no use by a minor is acceptable. You have the responsibility to manage your own family. Define what you believe is appropriate behavior for your children, according to each child's developmental level and unique strengths and weaknesses.

But you need to set realistic limits for yourself as well. Just as you cannot control your adolescent's behavior, you cannot take responsibility for it either. Taking control of and responsibility for your own behavior is difficult enough. You can not and should not spend your life covering up for, apologizing for, or making amends for an adolescent who chooses to behave irresponsibly.

Try to accept the simple fact that rescuing or protecting your child from his own bad choices hurts much more than it helps. This is very hard for loving, well-meaning parents to accept. It seems as though you should do anything in your power to help a child who's in trouble. So you run to school when the principal threatens to suspend your son for smoking. Or you rush to the police station and smooth things over when your daughter is picked up for underage drinking. But in these cases, helping won't help. It will just make your child even more irresponsible and resentful.

Rescuing your child from the consequences of her bad choices makes you an "enabler" of her drug-dependent behavior. Don't be. If your daughter gets thrown off the basketball team for drinking at a school function, resist the urge to go to the coach and try to talk him out of it. If your son loses car privileges because he went to a party where drinking occurred, don't back down just because he has tickets to a concert and no one else can drive.

Drugs and alcohol can become the most important source of pleasure and satisfaction in a young person's life. When drugs give such pleasure, and especially if they don't seem to be associated with any difficulty for the user, he resists giving them up. He thinks, "Why should I?" Only when drugs bring painful consequences will the user get motivated to abandon them.

Ultimately you cannot control whether your adolescent uses drugs. You can only decide what you will do if you find out, make the sanctions clear in advance, and follow through consistently.

Setting a Good Example

If you yourself use drugs or alcohol to "deal with stress," to "have fun with the guys," or to "forget about everything for a while," you may need to seek out a self-help support group for yourself. If someone else in your family abuses alcohol or drugs, join Al-Anon. Groups like Alateen provide a wonderful source of information and support for children in alcoholic families (see Resources).

Sticking to the Treatment Plan

If your child uses drugs or alcohol, you will probably feel guilty. You may have made some mistakes. You may not have set firm enough limits, and you may have been a bad example at times. But dwelling on the past won't solve a problem in the present. All you can do is simply do the best you can now. Take charge of your own behavior and don't cripple your child further by letting guilt make you assume responsibility that isn't yours.

Learn where and how to get treatment. For example, find out whether your schools have Student Assistance Programs to help children who are involved with drugs.

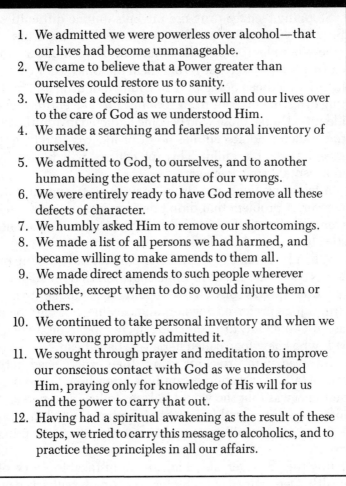

THE 12 STEPS

1. We admitted we were powerless over alcohol—that our lives had become unmanageable.
2. We came to believe that a Power greater than ourselves could restore us to sanity.
3. We made a decision to turn our will and our lives over to the care of God as we understood Him.
4. We made a searching and fearless moral inventory of ourselves.
5. We admitted to God, to ourselves, and to another human being the exact nature of our wrongs.
6. We were entirely ready to have God remove all these defects of character.
7. We humbly asked Him to remove our shortcomings.
8. We made a list of all persons we had harmed, and became willing to make amends to them all.
9. We made direct amends to such people wherever possible, except when to do so would injure them or others.
10. We continued to take personal inventory and when we were wrong promptly admitted it.
11. We sought through prayer and meditation to improve our conscious contact with God as we understood Him, praying only for knowledge of His will for us and the power to carry that out.
12. Having had a spiritual awakening as the result of these Steps, we tried to carry this message to alcoholics, and to practice these principles in all our affairs.

Most outpatient and inpatient drug programs are based on the 12-step program developed by Alcoholics Anonymous and adapted by groups from Narcotics Anonymous to Overeaters Anonymous. By "working" the 12 steps, your drug-dependent teenager will learn to see her dependence as a disease. She can then focus her energy on learning to resist the urge to drink or do drugs.

Stopping teenage drug use presents unique difficulties. Because your child has acquired a need to use drugs to relieve boredom, avoid discomfort, or overcome fear, you can expect him to resist giving them up. Since your child's identity has been developing in a milieu of drug use, quitting drugs means your teenager must form an entirely new identity. Unlike those who become addicted in adulthood, the addicted adolescent has no prior identity to return to except that of a child. This, of course, will be totally unacceptable to a teenager.

Adolescents who use drugs may take a long time to recover. A problem that didn't develop in a day or a week won't resolve itself quickly either. You need to be patient, stick to your guns, and take one day at a time.

When Joan came to see me, her parents had given up on her as a lost cause. The juvenile court referred the 16-year-old after she was convicted of stealing to get money to buy drugs. Joan preferred downers and cocaine, but she would use just about any drug she could get her hands on. In fact, kids who knew Joan called her a "garbage-head."

Involved with drugs for years, Joan experienced both school failure and abusive family relationships. Joan's biggest fear was that she would fail, so, following a perverse logic, she did everything within her power to fail miserably. Then she would cover up her resulting shame by using drugs.

But the teenager also had an unmistakable spark of health. Determined to get better, Joan finally embarked on the difficult path to recovery. She flitted in and out of treatment for a couple of years. Sometimes she lived at home and sometimes she stayed in a shelter. Although she remained clean for gradually increasing periods, Joan suffered several relapses. But the resolute young woman never gave up and I never gave up on her. Even at her lowest point, Joan maintained the conviction that she could be someone. Many kids as addicted as Joan never recover, but Joan eventually did.

Joan is now a junior in college, and she hasn't used drugs or alcohol in three years. She works hard on her studies in business administration, she holds a part-time job, and she still attends her AA meetings. She usually sends me a card during the holidays to let me know how she's doing. The last one ended with, "and I'm still clean and sober, Doc. It's not always the easiest thing, but it's the best thing that ever happened to me."

III

HELPING YOUR DEPRESSED CHILD

—

7

Suicide Prevention

Laura's grandfather died suddenly last year. An ambulance took him away in the middle of the night and his granddaughter never saw him alive again.

Laura had been closer to her grandfather than to anyone else in her family. Every afternoon after school the little girl would go to his apartment, where he played the piano while she sang and danced. Laura's divorced mother worked long hours in her beauty shop, often coming home late to find Laura and her grandfather asleep side by side on the couch with a storybook nearby.

After her grandfather died, the desperately lonely child was very depressed and frequently thought about joining him. Laura was 8 years old when she attempted suicide, jumping from a third-floor window in her apartment building.

You probably can't imagine your child attempting suicide. Very few parents can. Yet a quarter of a million children and adolescents try to kill themselves every year and more than 5,000 of them succeed.

Experts agree that both childhood and adolescent suicide go underreported, perhaps by as much as half. In fact, many of the accidents which are the primary cause of death in young people probably result from intentional self-harm. Most suicide attempts and many so-called accidents have a close link with depression.

Acknowledging the seriousness of the problem is the first step toward doing something about it. If you recognize that your depressed child or adolescent is at risk for suicide, you can prepare yourself to anticipate the danger and respond effectively.

THE SCOPE OF THE PROBLEM

In the United States in 1989, suicide claimed the lives of 4,870 young people between the ages of 15 and 24, and 240 children between 5 and 14. This preventable tragedy is now the third most common cause of death for 15-to-24-year-olds, following accidents and homicide, and the sixth most common cause of death for children ages 5 to 14. Over the past three decades, suicide rates have more than doubled for children 10 to 14. They've more than tripled for 15-to-19-year-olds.

The suicide rate for adolescents is 20 times that of children, perhaps because of the multiple pressures teens encounter. Many strive to succeed academically and athletically, and most want desperately to be popular. The stresses of building and dissolving intimate, sometimes sexual, relationships loom much greater than they do for younger children. Teens may feel compelled to drink, to use drugs, or to engage in illegal activities.

Along with the considerable pressure of these sometimes dangerous urges, adolescents experience considerably less support and supervision outside the home from their parents than younger children do. Partly because they are also striving for autonomy, adolescents usually communicate

less with their parents. As a result, parents may be completely ignorant about the stresses their adolescents face.
Teens' increased mobility brings exposure to many more
means of suicide than younger children encounter. All
these factors probably contribute to the increased frequency of suicide as children reach adolescence.

Access to fatal means such as guns plays a crucial role in
this equation. Comparing a group of adolescents who
attempted suicide to a control group, researchers at the
University of Pittsburgh discovered that guns were twice as
likely to be found in the homes of the suicidal teenagers.
The national school-based Youth Risk Behavior Survey
sponsored by the Centers for Disease Control found that
more than 27 percent of American high school students
had thought about suicide in the past 12 months, and that 4
percent of high school students—half a million teenagers—regularly carried a gun.

WHO IS AT GREATEST RISK?

Take a few minutes to answer the following questions
about your child:

1. How old is your child?
2. What gender is your child?
3. Has your child suffered the recent loss of a close
   friend or relative due to death, divorce, separation,
   or a move?
4. Does your child have a chronic or painful physical
   illness?
5. Is your child socially isolated?
6. Does your child feel unliked?
7. Is your child doing poorly in school?
8. Is there considerable conflict in your family?
9. Is your child angry or aggressive?
10. Is your child impulsive?

11. Is your child uncommunicative?
12. Is your child perfectionistic?
13. Does your child hear voices or have other psychotic symptoms?
14. Does your child use drugs or alcohol?
15. Does your child have access to a means of killing himself?
16. Does your child have a friend or relative who has committed suicide?
17. Has your child threatened or attempted suicide?

Here's how to interpret your answers to the above questions:

Age Older children attempt and complete suicide much more often than younger children. One theory suggests that the hormonal surge at puberty for both boys and girls contributes to an increased incidence of depression in this age group. Older children, especially older adolescents, can more easily plan a method of suicide and then carry it out.

Gender Three times more girls than boys attempt suicide, but three times more boys die. That's because boys usually choose more fatal methods with less chance of rescue for themselves. No one knows for sure why boys and girls differ this way. Male-female differences in total sex hormone levels or learning helplessness as part of their gender identity may make girls more susceptible to depression. And the male hormones that make boys more prone to aggressiveness may affect their choice of more violent and therefore more fatal means of suicide.

Loss Like many teenage suicides, Ken tried to kill himself after his girlfriend told him she wanted to date other boys. Seemingly less crucial losses can have similar effects, whether the losses are real, imagined, or only threatened. When a person loses physical health, competence, vigor, or something to live for, he must be considered at higher risk for depression and suicide.

In childhood and adolescence, the loss of a parent frequently precedes suicide. Dr. Michael Rutter spent several years studying children whose mothers had died. In *Depression in Young People* (Guilford Press, 1986), Rutter speculated about the many ways such a loss could contribute to depression, either immediately or years later.

A catastrophic loss might produce an immediate depression, called "anaclitic." In orphanages years ago, researchers observed babies as young as 6 months who were weeping, withdrawn, apathetic, and who displayed problems with sleeping and weight gain. Untreated, anaclitic depression can be fatal.

Though early catastrophic loss may have no immediate effects, it may alter a child's self-concept or style of interpreting the world forever. Early loss could prompt behavioral changes that might contribute to depression in later life. Subtle but persistent neuroendocrine changes could also trigger a delayed depression.

An early loss may sensitize a child to future losses by disturbing her coping mechanisms. If the loss negatively affects a child's selection of later relationships, she might unknowingly set herself up for further bereavement and depression.

A parent's intentional absence through abandonment or divorce can be even more traumatic to a child than the parent's death. The abandoned child may feel guilty, as though she'd done something to cause her parent to leave.

Physical Illness Dee had managed her diabetes quite well for years. But when she entered high school, she started to reduce her insulin and intentionally gorge herself on high-calorie foods. The 14-year-old was finally admitted to the hospital, near death in diabetic crisis.

Chronic illness or disability, major surgery, or deprivation of any important physical function can leave a child feeling defective, discouraged, and scared. Chronically ill adolescents may be at special risk because their age-appropriate drive toward independence often conflicts with their medical needs.

Social Isolation   Carol, 16, said, "I feel like a fifth wheel in my family. Everyone else seems to have a place and my younger brothers get all the love." Such isolation can leave a child vulnerable to depression and suicidal behavior.

Suicidal adolescents and children frequently describe a sense of being emotionally cut off from other family members. Maintaining that their parents seem to have "no time to listen," they feel that no one in their family cares for them. Suicidal teens talk about "holding it all in" or "keeping my problems to myself." But when they finally venture to let things out, they often discover the immense relief of talking with a concerned listener.

In meeting with the parents of these suicidal youngsters, I have often found that many are as isolated as their children, perhaps because they have recently moved or are too busy or troubled to develop a network of close friends.

Rejection   David cut his wrists after his mother kicked him out of the house and changed all the locks. Suicide attempts often follow such a rejection. In some families, the rejection is real: suicidal children report that their parents have said such things as "We'd all be better off without you," "You're worthless," "You're not needed or wanted here," or even "Go ahead and kill yourself—we won't even miss you."

Since depressed children are particularly vulnerable to rejection, even a minor slight can precipitate a suicide attempt. Such a child may perceive overt rejection in a situation where parents are merely preoccupied with work or their own marital conflict.

School Failure   Learning difficulties and failure at school can erode a child's self-esteem. Don, who attempted suicide at 9, reported that he was constantly teased and criticized by his classmates.

Some highly intelligent, competitive, perfectionistic children cannot tolerate any failure. Their self-hatred after seemingly small academic disappointments may be deadly. Failures that seem trivial to parents or teachers are unforgivable in the eyes of such a child. Julie killed herself in her junior year of high school after her English teacher discovered she had plagiarized parts of her term paper.

Family Conflict   Suicide attempts by children frequently follow violent family arguments. Indeed, the homes of suicidal children are often filled with conflict. In some cases, alcoholism or other drug abuse contributes to the atmosphere of mental or physical strife.

Anger and Aggression   Though a history of violence increases a child's risk for suicide, the suicidal child is usually not the only angry person in his family. Researchers have observed considerable family hostility directed toward the suicidal member as well.

Parents may display anger in a variety of ways. They might ignore or neglect their child or expose him to potentially dangerous situations. Some parents allow their child to become entangled in inappropriate relationships. Or they may simply allow their child to fail in school beyond a point where he can salvage the situation.

Parental anger and aggression might come out as gratuitous insults or constant reminders of the child's inadequacies. For example, Ellen's mother always told her, "You have nothing but your looks; when your looks go, you'll be nothing." Other parents physically assault their children with beatings, wounds, or sexual advances.

Susan was hospitalized on the day of her 15th birthday. The night before, she had swallowed every pill she could find in the medicine cabinet. About a year earlier, Susan's stepfather had begun sexually molesting her while her mother was at work. After hearing a talk on sexual abuse at school, Susan gathered the courage to tell her mother. The girl was shocked when her mother refused to believe her, called her a liar, and accused her of trying to break up the marriage. As the fight escalated, Susan's mother told her everyone would be better off if Susan had never been born. When Susan said she felt like killing herself, her mother told her to go ahead and save everyone a lot of trouble.

Susan stayed in the adolescent psychiatric unit for over a month. When she left the hospital, Susan continued at her old school because of a teacher she respected and many close friends. But the girl wisely chose to move out of her mother's house to a new home with an older cousin and an aunt.

Impulsivity   When a child tends to act quickly, without considering the consequences, the stage is set for a dangerous physical expression of depressed feelings and self-hatred. Youngsters who have not yet learned to recognize and label their feelings may be driven to dangerous or even irreversible behavior. The younger and more immature the child, the greater the tendency to act out anger, frustration, and disappointment.

Communicating by behavior instead of words, the suicidal child acts out the message, "I'm lonely and frightened and I don't know what to do. I'm mad at myself and at you, and I either want things to change or I want to get away from it all."

Impulsivity correlates closely with suicide attempts in both children and adolescents. Suicide attempts may be a spur-of-the-moment reaction to a temporary problem that might resolve itself given time and patience. Transient changes in friendships, disappointments in school or athletics, short-lived fights with family or friends—all can trigger suicidal behavior in impulsive youngsters.

Communication Difficulties   Family rules of communication sometimes prohibit open discussion of thoughts and feelings. When secretiveness is an unspoken family policy, parents may simply ignore their children's communications, even suicide threats and self-destructive behaviors.

Secretiveness is the rule in families where sexual abuse or alcoholism exists. Suicide itself generally takes place as a secretive act. What's more, this act usually guarantees that the victim's thoughts and feelings will never really become known.

Kim described her parents this way: "My father never talks and I never know what he's thinking. He just goes out to the garage all the time and works on his car. My mother talks all the time, but she never says anything. They don't talk to each other, except through me. I got sick of it and I just stopped talking, too."

Kim unplugged the telephone in her room, stopped calling or talking to her friends, and spent most of her time alone in her room. She stopped eating or drinking anything but diet cola and eventually dwindled to less than 80 pounds. Maintaining their denial that Kim had a serious problem, her parents skipped counseling appointments. Then Kim took a massive overdose of her mother's tranquilizers.

Every family operates according to unwritten, unspoken, unacknowledged rules of communication. These rules determine who may say what to whom, when, and under what circumstances. Such unwritten rules might include any of the following:

"Never admit to bad feelings."

"Always say that everything is fine."

"Never admit that you are confused, afraid, or depressed."

"Talk about your successes only with Dad; talk about failures only with Mom."

"All children communicate through Mom."

"If you must speak, say something critical."

"Girls will talk about their feelings with Mother; boys will not talk about feelings with anybody."

"Mother is fragile and any negative comments may
crush her."
"Daddy is uninvolved and will only listen and get involved if a child criticizes or attacks Mom."

Perfectionism   Jane was a tall, slender, musically talented
17-year-old. Intellectually gifted as well, Jane came from a
family of achievers. She had always lived up to their high
expectations.

In one month, Jane experienced a rapid succession of
what anyone else might have perceived as expectable failures. Her school's orchestra didn't make state finals, she
was passed over for the lead in the school play, and she got a
C in an important course. These failures sent Jane into a
suicidal depression.

Psychosis   Psychotic symptoms include hearing voices or
seeing visions that aren't real (hallucinations) and believing irrational ideas such as that one's thoughts are being
broadcast aloud to the world (delusions). The more severe
the child's mental disorder, the greater the risk of suicide.

Drugs and Alcohol   Abuse of drugs or alcohol increases a
young person's risk of committing suicide. These substances impair judgment, remove inhibitions to behavior,
and promote reckless or self-destructive acts. In their book
A Cry for Help (Doubleday, 1983), Mary Giffin and Carol
Felsenthal revealed that nearly half the adolescents who
commit suicide are drunk or high when they do it. And
more than 85 percent of the adolescents who attempt
suicide do so under the influence of drugs or alcohol.

Means   Having a convenient means, such as a revolver in a
dresser drawer, increases a child's risk. Remember that
childhood suicide is often an impulsive act, a response
to feelings of loneliness, frustration, and helplessness
that will soon pass. Parents of depressed children should

remove weapons from their house and should secure all medications.

Suicide by Friend or Relative   Nearly half of adolescents who attempt suicide have relatives or close friends who committed suicide. One-fourth of these were parents. Exposure to a suicide in the family may give a child the idea that it is a legitimate solution to life's problems.

Martin, 16, attempted to kill himself by cutting his wrists. His parents later found a noose tied in a clothesline in his closet. Even so, they denied the seriousness of his suicidal intention and demanded to take him home from the hospital against medical advice. In a meeting that included the extended family, Martin's parents revealed that four of the eight family members present in the room had themselves attempted suicide in the past. Martin, his mother, his uncle, his grandmother, and his grandfather had all tried to kill themselves, some more than once.

Suicide Threats and Prior Attempts   Contrary to popular myth, previous attempts and talk about suicide do not mean a child will not actually commit suicide. Adolescents who attempt suicide almost always give some warning. And most completed suicides have been preceded by at least one attempt. Never ignore, contradict, or belittle a suicide threat. You need to intervene immediately.

SOMETIMES YOU CAN'T TELL

Not every suicide attempt advertises itself with warning signals such as gestures, threats, or notes. Occasionally, a child who kills himself has never given the slightest hint that he is depressed. Michael, for example, was a popular, successful, seemingly happy 12-year-old. Until the day he killed himself with his father's shotgun, no one had any reason to suspect Michael was depressed.

Like Michael, some suicidal children do not appear to be markedly depressed or even unhappy. But due to stress, a lack of personal support, inadequate coping skills, and the availability of means, these children find an answer in suicide.

WHY CHILDREN AND ADOLESCENTS SAY THEY WANT TO KILL THEMSELVES

A child decides to commit suicide because she feels hopeless about her future and powerless to change herself or her world. Children usually attempt suicide in the midst of a crisis, such as the loss of a relative or friend, or a failure—academic, athletic, or social. The suicidal child believes there are only two choices in the situation: to live in suffering or to die.

This type of constricted, either-or thinking characterizes all depression, but is especially pronounced in children, who haven't yet developed the ability to perceive shades of gray or to recognize a continuum of possible solutions. Combine this black-and-white thinking style with the tendency to prefer black, and you can understand why childhood depression sometimes leads to suicide.

I asked children in my practice why they had tried to commit suicide. Many said they had actually been calling for help. Linda answered, "I wanted my parents to notice that I had problems, real problems, and I wanted them to do something about it. I guess I wanted help, but I couldn't just ask for it. That seemed impossible. I didn't think they'd listen. I didn't think they'd take it seriously."

Childhood victims of physical or sexual abuse often attempt suicide as a last-ditch effort to escape their pain, fear, and suffering. Other children seek an escape from chaotic family lives. Jon, whose parents fought all the time, said, "I didn't want to worry about anything anymore. I just wanted to be somewhere very quiet."

Sometimes revenge or punishment provides a motive—to make a parent or friend suffer. Sandy said, "I was furious at all of them—my parents, my best friend, the whole world, really. I wanted to get back at them, to cause them as much pain as they had caused me."

Or suicide may be a sacrifice, an effort to take on the guilt or problems of an entire family. Josh was 9 years old and often visited the emergency room for episodes of asthma medication overdose. When we asked Josh what was worrying him, he said he was concerned about his mother, who suffered from hypertension and asthma. Josh frequently lay awake in bed at night for hours, listening to his mother wheeze and gasp for air. Afraid she would die, he didn't have the courage to tell her how frightened he was. But when Josh took an overdose of her medication, the emergency room staff noticed *her* wheezing and treated her as well. The little boy had found a dangerous way of getting help for his mother.

Some suicide attempts, like 8-year-old Laura's, stem from a wish to join a loved one in the afterlife or an attempt to undo a painful loss through death. In these cases, suicide may seem to promise an escape from unbearable suffering.

Joe's father hanged himself at the peak of a financial crisis he didn't believe he could survive. The boy, who loved him dearly, could never forget the sight of his father dangling from a pipe in the basement. Joe thought frequently of joining his father in death and even dreamed about being with him again. Two years later, on the anniversary of his father's death, the 15-year-old hanged himself.

Many children and teens have told me they hurt themselves in order to gain attention, sympathy, or remorse. Nancy thought her parents didn't pay enough attention to her. She said, "I wanted my parents to notice I was alive." Tim was devastated when his girlfriend broke up with him. He said, "I wanted her to feel sorry for me."

Scott took a knife to his arm in order to test his mother's love. "I wanted to see how she would react. I wanted her to see me with the knife and say, 'No, don't do it, Scott, don't hurt yourself. I love you; I don't want you to die.'" Unfortunately, his mother didn't say that. When she saw him with the knife she turned and walked away from him in disgust. Then he attempted suicide by cutting himself.

Suicide may be a drastic effort by a child who feels she has lost control over outside events. Leslie said, "I didn't want my boyfriend to break up with me. . . . I thought he might not leave me if he thought it would kill me. I thought he would come back to me when he knew I was in the hospital for attempted suicide."

Cluster Suicides

Several communities have been devastated by what have been called "cluster suicides" or "copycat suicides." In one town a well-liked seventh-grader began the cascade by suddenly and inexplicably hanging himself in the local park. Some people speculated he was imitating a suicide depicted in a popular movie. Ten days later another teen hanged himself in a nearby forest preserve. Within two days, a 19-year-old had shot himself, and within another week, two more teens had hanged themselves. The horror finally ended, but only after another 19-year-old had asphyxiated himself with carbon monoxide.

Copycat suicides by unacquainted youths puzzle experts. Perhaps a complete coincidence, these events likely represent a trigger phenomenon in which the suicidal behavior of an already vulnerable person gets set off by example.

Suicide can't always be predicted in advance. But you should consider any of the 12 warning signs described on page 143 a red flag.

THE 12 WARNING SIGNS OF SUICIDE

1. Personality change: a gregarious child becomes withdrawn or a shy child becomes extremely outgoing.
2. Disregard for appearance: an adolescent who is normally scrupulous about how he looks suddenly begins to neglect his grooming, hygiene, and clothing.
3. Social withdrawal.
4. Giving away treasured possessions and putting affairs in order.
5. Preoccupation with death or morbid themes, including rock music, drawings, poems, and essays.
6. Overt or veiled suicide threats: "I won't be around much longer." "They'd be better off without me." "I wish I were dead."
7. Prior suicide attempts.
8. Acquisition of a means (ropes, guns, hoses).
9. Substance abuse.
10. School failure.
11. Sudden elevation of mood in a depressed child. This may mean your depressed child has found a "solution"—suicide.
12. Increased accidents or multiple physical complaints with no medical basis.

WHAT YOU CAN DO

If your child displays any of these signs or if you're worried about suicide for any other reason, take some time to sit down in a quiet place with your child and talk about your concerns. You may feel hesitant to do this or fearful of what you might hear.

You need to know that *talking about suicide will not plant an idea in a child who isn't suicidal and it won't cause suicide in one who is.* Avoiding the subject can prove much more dangerous.

Here are some questions you might ask your child:

Has something been bothering you a lot lately?
Have you been depressed about it? For how long?
Have you been feeling angry and irritable?
Do you have someone you can talk to about the things that bother you?
Do you feel comfortable talking to me about it?
Do you ever feel so bad that you think you'd be better off dead?
Do you ever think about killing yourself?
Have you made a plan about how you would kill yourself?
Have you ever tried to hurt yourself or kill yourself before?
Have you ever known anyone who killed himself?
What do you imagine death would be like?
What do you think our family would be like if you were gone?
How do you think I would feel if you killed yourself?
Is there anything you look forward to in the future?
Do you really want to die?

The child who expresses suicidal thoughts is not a lost cause. Suicide is *not* inevitable. Suicidal thoughts represent a child's failure to conceive of a better solution to a serious problem. As a parent, you can help your child find a better solution. Your commitment to your child can help her find her way out of a temporary dilemma.

Struggles and disappointments at school, with friends, or in extracurricular activities are extremely important to children and adolescents. They need to know that you appreciate the gravity of their concerns. So let your child tell you in her own words, in her own time, how her life is going. Encourage her to tell you what she fears, what she worries about, what she likes and what she hates—even about you or the things you cherish.

Let her talk about thoughts or feelings that are frightening, embarrassing, or irrational to you or to her. Allow her to express her thoughts and feelings without judging them.

Tell your child how you feel about her, how much you love her and how much you would miss her if she were gone. Tell her what *you* fear and what *you* worry about. Tell her what it was like for you when you were her age and about times you felt frustrated, angry, fearful, or depressed.

If your child says she wishes she were dead, or that others would be better off without her, believe her. She is serious and she is in trouble if she can think of no better way out than to threaten or actually attempt to hurt herself. Listen carefully without arguing or telling your child "It's not that bad." It *is* that bad, to her. Accept her feelings and tell her you can imagine how horrible she must feel to think of taking her own life. Assure her you'll be there for her and that you'll share the problem and try to help her in any way you can.

Emphasize that while most problems are temporary, suicide is permanent. Try to lend your child an adult's perspective on life's problems—that even overwhelming problems can often be solved.

Your child's hopelessness allows her to envision no possibilities other than death. Show your child how to think about her problems, how to take another perspective, how to imagine many approaches to a solution. There's never just one way or just one right way. Think, talk it over, and think some more. Struggle along with your child, sharing your reasons for believing that things can get better and your child can have a satisfying and happy life even in this imperfect world. By doing this, you'll be giving her a model for problem-solving as well as for personal competence. You will convey the conviction that problems can be solved.

Explore how your child's depression developed and try to understand how things got to their present state of desperation. Recognize and accept your child's feelings and your own feelings. You can't simply stop feeling bad about something, but you'll feel better if you can find a way to solve the problem, change yourself, or change the situation.

When a child expresses despair and thoughts of suicide, he needs help protecting his own life. Your child is your responsibility and his life is in your hands. You must take over for him temporarily. You'll need to stay with him and to arrange adequate supervision when you can't be there. Don't leave him alone while he feels like hurting himself. Remove guns, knives, razors, ropes, pills, and poisons from your house until you are sure the threat of suicide has passed.

Whatever else you do, don't bear this burden alone—that is exactly what your suicidal child has been trying to do. Demonstrate to your child how to ask for help and how to depend on other people. Share the responsibility with your spouse, other relatives, and close friends. Get help from your family doctor, your local mental health clinic, or a crisis line. To find the closest suicide-prevention center, call 911, O, 411, your local police, or look in the Yellow Pages under Mental Health, Counseling, Suicide, or Crisis. You might start by calling a meeting of family and friends closest to your child. Invite your clergyperson and your child's teacher—anyone who has an interest in your child and is willing to get involved and help.

Whether or not your own child is suicidal, suicide prevention is a community affair. Mrs. Anderson consulted me because she had three teenagers living at home, each boasting five or ten good friends, and the Andersons' most recent telephone bill featured multiple phone calls to a suicide crisis hotline. When Mrs. Anderson asked her children about it, they all said they didn't know anything. Now Mrs. Anderson couldn't sleep because she knew someone was contemplating suicide, but she didn't know who it could be.

I suggested she share her concerns at a meeting of her family and friends. The Anderson children agreed to invite their friends to the meeting, too. The day after the meeting, the mystery caller confided to Mrs. Anderson's younger son that he was depressed and thinking about suicide. After the meeting, he finally felt safe enough to tell someone about it. Following brief therapy, he's currently alive and well and enjoying his senior year in high school.

8

ALL IN THE FAMILY: HELPING YOURSELF AND YOUR CHILD

When Sally attempted suicide, our whole family was forced to take a hard look at itself," acknowledged the mother of a 13-year-old. "Sally had always been our 'perfect' child—good grades, lots of activities and friends, my best helper—and we had prided ourselves on being the perfect family, too. Sally's depression delivered the brutal message that we had a serious family problem."

In some cases a depressed child seems to be reacting to a depressed parent or a distressed family situation. But even when depression appears to come out of the blue, as in Sally's case, it affects the entire family. Think of your family as a mobile. The position of each family member influences the whole balance, so the movement of one member naturally triggers change in the rest of the system.

Having a depressed child will certainly force you to look deeply at yourself. Sally's mother said, "I have never questioned myself so much as I did in the first days after her suicide attempt. I kept asking myself, 'Where did I go wrong?' "

A depressed child, especially one who does not seem to get better in spite of your best efforts, can make you doubt your parental skills. In fact, your self-esteem as a parent may well mirror your child's low self-esteem.

Unfortunately, since self-esteem motivates much of what we do, this problem can perpetuate itself. Hundreds of activities compete for our time and attention each day. Naturally, we tend to do things that make us feel good about ourselves and to avoid whatever makes us feel bad. Parenting a depressed child who can't be cheered up may be so hard on your self-esteem that you unconsciously begin to avoid your child. But avoiding her will only make your problem worse.

A child's depression will probably affect you in other ways, too. As parents we tend to identify with our children and their struggles. When your child suffers a crisis, you may experience the problem as if it were your own, especially if it repeats a similar plight from your own past. Part of helping your child may even involve reworking some of your own childhood problems. For example, Sally's mother said: "I had always been a lonely child, and I prided myself on Sally's active social life. When she tried to kill herself I saw for the first time that perhaps inside Sally felt just as lonely as I always did."

Indeed, your child's depression may pose both a risk and an opportunity for you. The risk is that you will be brought down by your child's problem and experience a depression of your own. On the other hand, helping your child through her depression may actually help you resolve some long-buried childhood issues.

How you react to your child's depression will depend on many factors, including your own background and your previous relationship to your child. But most parents of depressed children experience very similar feelings. You may find it a relief to discover that you share these emotions with other parents.

After describing the normal feelings the parents of depressed children experience, we offer some observations on fathers and siblings for these often-neglected family members. Once you have faced up to your feelings about having a depressed child, you will need to jump in with both feet to help your child. The last half of this chapter will show you how to do exactly that.

NORMAL PARENTAL FEELINGS

Denial

Awareness of your child's problems can prove extremely painful. To protect themselves from this pain, many parents simply deny their child's depression. The father of a depressed 9-year-old admitted, "It was right in front of our eyes and we just didn't want to let ourselves see it. Clay was miserable and unhappy for months. He had something to cry about every day. He wanted to quit his soccer team and his guitar lessons; he had simply lost interest in everything. My wife sensed something was wrong, but she figured the teacher was boring, or the coach was too hard on him, or the other kids were picking on him. I kept telling her Clay was just lazy. We were both seeing it the way we wanted to see it, instead of the way it really was. Now we know Clay was really depressed, and that's a terrible thing for a child."

Guilt

As parents we wrestle with guilt and doubt all the time: Do I spend enough time with my kids? Will it hurt them to be in day care while I work? Am I traveling too much or at home too little? If I don't let them go to every party, will they end up lonely and miserable?

When depression strikes a child, parents typically express guilt over issues and concerns that they already felt sensitive about. A successful real estate broker whose 7-year-old was in therapy for depression put it this way: "I blame myself. I had always wanted children, and I planned to stay home with them full-time while they were growing up. I stayed home with Kerri for five and a half years and she was fine, a normal happy child. But I wanted more for myself. I felt as if I might never have a career if I waited any longer. I went into real estate because I thought I could make my own hours, but that was a joke. My hours are all hours. I'm good at what I do, and it's nice to see results and to have other people, other adults, appreciate my work. But Kerri definitely gets left on her own a lot. I made a choice, but now that I see what's happened, I think I was wrong."

Anger

Although it doesn't seem rational, you may well feel angry at your depressed child. But anger will only add to your guilt as you wonder, "How can I be mad at this poor sick child?" The mother of a depressed 13-year-old said, "Cindy was terribly depressed, but she didn't seem to want to do anything about it, and that made me mad. I was trying everything I could think of to cheer her up and she just rejected everything. She wouldn't even try. I know now that that's part of the illness, but I was so mad at her then. Of course, as soon as I got mad at her I'd start feeling guilty. She'd just take it, like she thought she deserved it, so I'd get mad at myself and feel worse, and then pretty soon I'd be mad at her again. It was awful."

You may well feel frustrated at not being able to say the

"right things" to get through to your child. One father said, "I couldn't motivate Tim or help him feel better about himself. This made me feel all the angrier at him for not trying at school and for just giving up when he had so much going for him."

To protect yourself from your guilt-producing anger, you may direct it toward another family member. You might pick a fight with your spouse, for example. Or you might join together to blame your child's school or doctor.

Such projection spares you from getting angry at your child and blaming yourself, but it won't solve your problem. The father of an 11-year-old said, "When the school counselor called us in and said she thought Kevin was depressed, I got offended, wondering, 'How dare she say that about my son?' When it became pretty clear that something really was wrong, I blamed the school at first: They were putting too much pressure on him, and they weren't giving him the extra help he needed. I wasted a lot of time being angry and looking for someone to blame when I should have just accepted the fact that we had a problem and done something about it."

Confusion

If your child is depressed, you may feel bewildered and unable to identify your feelings. Penny, 8, fell into a deep depression after her family moved. Her mother said, "I just don't know what to do, I can't figure out how to help her. Nothing I say seems to make any difference. I remind her of all her wonderful qualities, all the things she's got going for her, but she doesn't care. I've never seen a child so unhappy and I just don't know what to do about it. I'm not that close to my family, and we just moved here so I don't even know who to talk with about it."

Grief

Having a depressed child may make you feel almost as if your real child had died. Indeed, you have lost every parent's fantasy of having the "perfect" child. Rob's father described it this way: "He was everything I ever wanted in a son: smart, good at sports, and he even liked to do the same things I like to do. I could have just as much fun with Rob as I could have with one of my friends. But now that's all gone. In fact, it's like the real Rob is gone. Now he doesn't want to do anything with me. He won't even look me in the eye." Rob's father broke down in tears as he sobbed, "I want my son back."

Shame

Our culture, schools, and neighborhoods often show little tolerance for an impaired child. No wonder the parents of a depressed child frequently anticipate social rejection, ridicule, or pity.

The father of a depressed 10-year-old said, "I feel sort of guilty saying this, but it got to the point where I was ashamed for people to see Eric. We'd go places like a school picnic or to a big family get-together, and all the other kids would be running around playing and he'd just sit by himself like a lump. At first the kids would try to get him involved, but then they'd give up and sort of avoid him. Anybody could look at Eric and see there was something wrong with him."

Other parents may not want their children playing with your depressed child. They may not care to hear about your struggles either, perhaps because of their own fears. Parents of depressed children frequently talk about feeling cut off from their families and others. You may feel you have no one to turn to.

Depression

It's not hard to understand why your child's depression would make you feel sad. Trying to help your child and getting no response can be exhausting and demoralizing. Sarah's father said, "I can't deal with all this. I've got tremendous pressure on me at work; it never lets up. When I come home, Sarah is crying about everything. She says she has no friends and wishes she were dead. I just can't handle it. I feel as if I have nothing left to say, nothing to give."

The mother of a depressed 15-year-old said, "Alice is so negative about everything, so convinced that nothing will work out, it's beginning to rub off on me. I'm feeling pretty pessimistic myself and I was always a positive person."

Fear

Having a depressed child can make you feel legitimately scared. You wonder what is going to happen to your child. You fear he may never get better or be happy again. You know that none of his friends wants to be around him and you wonder if he is going to be lonely like this from now on.

You may also have fears about your other children: If depression is partly genetic, will they get it too? Some parents recall an adult family member who has been depressed or has had emotional problems and speculate that their depressed child may turn out like these relatives. Parents who have been depressed themselves may be particularly worried that their child will end up like them.

Positive Feelings

Some parents find it a relief to finally have a diagnosis and the hope of help for their depressed child. For example,

during a discussion of his son's depression, one father remarked, "It's actually a relief to finally know what's
wrong, to have a name for it. For months we've been
worried sick about Pete, but he kept putting us off, telling
us nothing was wrong. We didn't know what was going on.
For a while we wondered about drug abuse, and another
time his mother started to imagine that he had a serious
physical illness, but we just didn't know what to think.
Now we've got something to go on. If we know what it is,
we can do something about it."

Indeed, acknowledging your child's depression may afford you a great sense of relief. Pam, 10, suffered from
depression and multiple developmental disabilities. After
several months of therapy, Pam's mother commented, "I've
always tried to sugarcoat everything, to make it all nice
and pleasant even if it isn't. Never until today would I
admit that I have a hard time dealing with my daughter.
I've been too afraid of what people would think of me. But
she does have problems, and I'm no longer ashamed to
admit it. Now I just want to do something about it."

FATHERS

Fathers of depressed children can't easily be categorized,
but in my clinical practice I frequently encounter two
distinct personalities. One is the critical, perfectionistic,
and overbearing father who rules his family with an iron
fist. The other is the distant father, who stays away from
home much of the time, or acts preoccupied when he is
there. A father who behaves in either of these ways may
well have a depressed wife as well as a depressed child.

Most fathers tend to participate less actively as parents
than mothers do, perhaps because their own fathers never
showed them how. Frequently fathers don't feel as competent at fathering as they do at their regular job. Indeed, the

working world discourages active fathering. But even if a couple decides that the mother will assume primary responsibility for day-to-day care of the children, all children require certain things from their fathers: demonstrations of love, time together, and acceptance.

Demonstrations of Love

Time and again my patients—depressed boys and girls and their parents—tell me, "I've never been close to my father. He doesn't really have much to do with me. He doesn't show his feelings."

As a father, you should let your child know you love him every single day. By this I don't mean that you simply make a rote comment. I mean you need to really look at your child and think about how much he means to you, then tell him. This means a lot and he'll remember it forever.

Time Together

The average American father spends less than 20 minutes a day with his children. Spending time together doesn't mean sitting in the family room reading the newspaper while your children watch television. It means having a meal together and talking, playing catch in the backyard, reading a bedtime story, or even running errands together on Saturday morning.

Acceptance

Too many depressed children, or adults who were depressed as children, feel that they were never good enough for their fathers. They say they never felt they measured up to his expectations. The father of a depressed child put it this way: "I never felt as though I pleased my father, never felt like a good enough son. When I went into business as a young man, I set goals for myself, but as soon as I achieved them I'd decide they were insignificant and set higher ones. I was never proud of myself. Now I have children and I don't feel like a good enough father."

You should set realistic and attainable goals for your children, just as you should set them for yourself. But you also need to accept your children for who they are so you can help them make the most of their unique talents.

BROTHERS AND SISTERS

The whole family mobile swings differently when a child gets depressed. Siblings may be affected in several ways. For example, a child's depression can escalate the pressure on his siblings to succeed. The younger sister of a depressed adolescent boy explained, "Jonathan screws up everything he does. I don't know if he *can't* do anything right, or he just doesn't try, or he doesn't want to. I think he doesn't try. Actually, I think he likes getting my parents ticked off. But then they just put more pressure on me. They keep telling me I'm not like him, that I have what it takes to be a success. But I don't know if I want to be a success. I don't think I can take the responsibility."

Sisters and brothers may feel burdened when the depressed child is treated specially. They may even feel guilty about being happy. Debbie, the twin sister of a depressed 12-year-old, said, "I'm actually a pretty happy person, but she's so unhappy, so down all the time, that I sort of hide it when I'm feeling good. I mean, if something good happens and I'm excited about it, when I see her I just feel guilty. I'm even afraid that my good mood will make her feel worse or something."

Misbehavior or acting depressed occasionally garners siblings some of the attention that gets bestowed upon their depressed sister or brother. The parents of a depressed 8-year-old noticed that whenever she would cry and complain that no one liked her at school, her 6-year-old brother would misbehave. If he made enough trouble, he could capture his mother's attention. His misbehavior also temporarily distracted his sister and mother from their own suffering.

Siblings may assume a premature independence, leaving their own needs unmet to defer to their depressed sister or brother. They may also worry about their friends' reactions, about how to communicate if their parents are trying to cover up, and about their own vulnerability to depression. Most of all, they wonder, "Will this happen to me?"

WHAT YOU CAN DO

Facing Facts

Before you can help your depressed child, you need to give up your denial and accept reality. Stop pretending that nothing is the matter or that your child will simply outgrow it.

You may also need to look squarely at your own contribution to your child's problems. For example, ask yourself whether you have put undue pressure on your son, pushing him to succeed at things that you failed at yourself. Or consider whether you have placed your daughter in an impossible situation, such as insisting that she side with you against your spouse in marital conflicts.

If your attitudes or behaviors have contributed to your child's problem, you may need to be willing to make some painful changes in yourself. It's particularly crucial to stop playing out problems with your spouse in your relation-

ships with your children. For example, if you're angry at
your husband for being gone too much, for being involved
too little, or for not helping you out enough, don't take it
out on your son by berating him for being lazy. If you're
angry at your wife for being overinvolved in her social life
and unavailable to you, don't automatically criticize your
daughter for spending too much time with her friends.
Begin to deal with your real problem and the right person.
Separate your own issues from your child's.

Letting Your Child Be Himself

Separating your concerns from your child's means that
when your child succeeds, he succeeds for himself, and
when he fails, he fails himself first. Children dislike feeling
pressured to achieve for their parents' gratification. They
also hate it when their parents act unduly upset over their
failures. A child needs to come to terms with his own
limitations and maintain his own self-esteem without having to worry about his parents. Go ahead and empathize
with your child's disappointments. But make sure you bear
in mind they're *his* disappointments. You're supposed to be
comforting your child, not expecting him to comfort you.

You may be tempted to shield your depressed child, to
try to protect him from negative experiences. But protec-
tiveness can quickly become the overprotectiveness that
leads to excessive dependency. At times you may simply
need to accept your child's sadness and allow him to work
it through. As one father put it, "If you want your children
to be happy, you'll have to accept a lot of their unhappy
feelings."

Doing the Right Thing

To do the right thing, you may well have to do the hard
thing. If your daughter's problems, such as being over-

weight or doing poorly at school, undermine her self-esteem and contribute to her depression, it's easy to lecture her: "You shouldn't eat so much junk food." "You should exercise more." "You need to spend more time on your homework." "You should check your math problems before you hand the assignment in." But nagging, the easy thing, usually proves to be the wrong thing.

It's harder but better to invest yourself in creating a context for success. Help your child set goals and come up with rewards for achieving them. For example, you might design an exercise and diet program and embark on it together. Or you could try to think of fun things to do together that would build fitness.

If homework is your daughter's problem, read a book like Lee Canter's *Homework Without Tears* (Harper-Collins, 1988), and create a place where she might actually like to study. Start by turning off the television and unplugging the phone for two hours every night. Then you can read and study with your child, instead of simply nagging her about it.

Getting Rid of Guilt

Nobody's a perfect parent. As parents, we're always doing most things for the first time, with no training and no rehearsal. No wonder we all make so many mistakes. But persecuting yourself for honest errors helps neither you nor your child. Simply acknowledge your failings and try doing things differently the next time.

Finding Help

Don't let embarrassment or denial prevent you from seeking help for yourself and your child (see Chapter 9). Most depressed American adults fail to get treatment for themselves. But depressed children depend on their parents to obtain therapy for them. Since your child is your responsibility, it's your job to make sure he gets the treatment he needs.

Getting to Know Your Child

If you don't know your child well, start learning about her now. Try to get acquainted without jumping to conclusions or making value judgments. Figure out what gets her worried or stressed out and what disappoints her the most.

You can't know what your child is proud of or struggling with unless you've visited her school, met her friends, seen her play softball, worked on math problems with her, listened to her music, and read a book that she particularly enjoyed.

Watch how your child walks, talks, and plays with other children. Get to know how she feels in different situations and what she thinks about things. Become acquainted with her friends and learn what she feels about them, why she likes them, and how her friendships are going.

Learn, too, what your child views as her greatest strengths and what she builds her self-esteem on. Disappointments in these areas will be most likely to precipitate your child's depression. Once you know your child well, you can be alert to the early signs of depression, and poised to help.

In addition to watching your child for signs of depression, don't forget to be liberal with sincere praise. Always be on the lookout for things to compliment about your child. Praise shows your child you're paying attention and it shows you appreciate her. Find something to celebrate about your child every day.

Spending Time Together

In order for kids to feel comfortable confiding in you, you need to be around them a lot. Your child needs to know that you are there for him, that you're on his side. It's not that you're taking his side against some other person—you're siding with him against his depression.

I'm skeptical about the recently popular notion of "quality time." It seems to imply that you don't have to spend much time with your kids as long as you jazz up the brief intervals you do spend with them.

I'm all for making the time you spend with your child a special period in which you are there completely for him, without distractions. But children talk only when they're ready to talk. And when they feel like discussing something important, you had better be there or you'll miss it.

Talking to Your Child

To know your child well, you'll have to talk to her. For the very young child, putting thoughts and feelings into words can be difficult. She may express many of her most important concerns through play (see Chapter 9 for ideas on how to play with your child).

Tell your older child what you've noticed, what you're concerned about, and what you think needs to be done. He may not like everything he hears you say, especially if he's been trying to pretend that he doesn't have a problem, but he'll probably respect you for saying what you think. Your child will probably also be glad that you've noticed what was going on with him.

GETTING STARTED   You might begin such a talk this way: "I noticed you haven't been interested in doing things with your friends lately, and you seem unhappy a lot of the time; what's wrong?"

Sometimes it helps to start a conversation by talking about neutral topics or areas in which your child excels. This can break the ice and help her feel more confident. Indeed, we all reveal our doubts and insecurities more readily if we feel strong and if we think the person talking to us recognizes our good points. Remember that it's as important for you and your child to recognize her strengths as it is to uncover her problems.

ASKING QUESTIONS   Asking questions assures that the focus of the conversation will remain on your child instead of becoming an opportunity for you to lecture or recite your own opinions about the topic at hand. Your questions should provide both an invitation for your child to speak and a means of drawing him into conversation. They should stimulate your child to consider things for himself.

On the other hand, some questions may feel like a cross-examination to your child. At times, questions carry too much of an implied demand for performance or seem to insist that your child reveal something he'd prefer to keep secret. For a beleaguered, defensive child, questions may be more than he can handle. In that situation, neutral statements may be less threatening and more conducive to further conversation: "It's just not the same around here since Grandpa died. I miss him." "It doesn't seem like you call Betsy as much as you used to." "You seem really tired when you come home from school these days."

You should also be careful asking "why," which may sound to your child like a demand for an explanation or an accusation. Children often don't know why, and you need to help them try to figure it out. You might do this by investigating their feelings at the time, by exploring the consequences of an action, or by looking at the reactions of people around them. For example, instead of asking, "Why did you pretend to have a stomachache to stay home from school?" you might ask something like: "Was something worrying you on Thursday morning when you complained about a stomachache and didn't want to go to school?" or "Did something happen in school the day before?"

Make sure you don't ask too many questions at once and that you don't simply rattle off one question after another like a prosecuting attorney. Think, too, about how you reacted to your child's stomachache and what you did. In fact, your reaction may have been the principal goal of your child's behavior.

It sometimes helps to say that other kids have thought or felt a certain way, even as you wonder about your child's feelings now. For example, you might say, "It's pretty common to be scared of moving to a new town" or "Most kids feel sad when they have to move away and leave their old friends."

Questions about the future can be liberating. Thinking about future possibilities can help you and your child get rid of the sense of being stuck with your problems. It also helps you both imagine and rehearse new alternatives.

Try asking questions like: "When you get used to our new neighborhood and your new school, do you think you'll want to join the band at school or at the community center?" "When you're not feeling so blue anymore, who do you think will be more relieved, your sister or your friend, Jill?" "Do you think you would have been more upset about breaking up with John three months ago or now? Now or three months from now? How upset do you think you'll feel about it three years from now?"

You also need to give your depressed child permission not to talk. If a child doesn't know the answer to a question, she should be allowed simply to say so. But sometimes if your child really doesn't know, you can suggest she take a guess. Her guess might tell you a lot about how she's thinking or feeling.

If your child knows but doesn't want to talk about it, she should be able to say, "I don't want to talk about that." Be prepared to wait, but be sure to let her know that you're available and interested. You might say, "I can tell that you don't feel like talking right now. I'll check in on you later or we can drive to school together tomorrow and talk then if you want."

Don't be too quick to conclude that your child doesn't want to talk. Sometimes a child needs to be coaxed, or simply wants you to sit and hang out with her for a while. As she gets more comfortable, she may become convinced that you really want to listen and that you haven't just allotted 10 minutes out of a sense of parental duty. For a serious talk, make sure you have plenty of time and won't be interrupted.

LISTENING   To get to know your child, you need to be willing to listen more than you talk. In fact, sometimes you don't even have to say anything, but can simply *be* with your child. Your mere presence offers comfort.

Listening is active communication, too, of course. It means working to understand what your child is saying, and struggling to imagine what he's feeling and why he feels that way. Listening actively and patiently tells your child that he is important and that you care about what he has to say.

Resist the natural temptation to interrupt, to correct, to jump in with advice, to try to convince your child his problem is not serious, or even to solve it for him. Suspend judgment and take the time to hear everything your child wants to say without correcting, telling him he doesn't really feel that way, or trying to make it better before you really understand what he's going through.

Listen for metaphors. Small children especially may express their feelings in the stories they tell and in how they interpret the things around them. A lonely little girl may tell you, for example, "My kitty is lonesome because her mother is gone and no one will play with her." Listen for similarities between the problems your child describes outside the home and difficulties that may exist in the family. If your 8-year-old constantly complains that her teacher doesn't listen to her and never has time to show her how to do the math problems, examine yourself. Do you make the time to help her with her homework? Do you take the time to really listen to her concerns?

Pay attention to what your child doesn't say, too. What isn't said can sometimes be the strongest communication of all. If your daughter suddenly stops talking about a best friend, for example, something is probably wrong, and she's probably feeling it.

TAKING YOUR CHILD SERIOUSLY   Your child's problems are vitally important to him. A 14-year-old's heartbreak over rejection by her boyfriend will make her feel the same way you would feel if you had been hurt by someone you loved. Deciding whether to compete on the swimming team or drop this activity for another can be agonizing. Don't brush off your child's confidences about these problems with comments such as, "Don't worry, you're still young," or "I'm sure everything will work out, honey." It may be hard for you to accept how strongly your child feels, but he needs for you to try. You can also help your child evaluate alternative solutions to his problems by predicting and weighing the consequences of various actions.

Listen attentively with all your senses for the feelings behind the words. Acknowledge your child's right to have strong feelings, negative as well as positive. Feelings themselves are neither good nor bad, right nor wrong. Feelings don't even have to be logical.

Never tell your child that he doesn't or shouldn't feel how he feels. Strong feelings often seem overwhelming, but you can help your child get control of them. Let's say your 13-year-old comes home from school, slams the front door, throws his backpack onto the table, scattering your papers to the floor, and barks, "Get off my case!" when you ask him to pick up your papers. You know something's bothering him, but you don't like being spoken to that way and you're tempted to let him have it.

Try to hold your own anger in check. Tell your child you don't like being talked to that way, but you can see something is really making him mad. Say, "How about instead of taking it out on me, tell me what's made you so mad and I'll see if I can help."

SHARING YOURSELF   A large part of communicating with children or anyone else is the reciprocal part, the mutual sharing of thoughts, feelings, and experiences. You might say, for example, "I'm confused; I can see you're unhappy but I don't know how to help."

Especially when you recognize that your child is going through something that you yourself have experienced, you can help her by telling her what it was like for you. You might say, for example, "I remember what I felt like when I didn't make the freshman basketball team. I felt like a loser. I felt like the guys who made it were better than me in every way, and as though it was some sort of final judgment, that they'd always be better than me after that." Or, "My parents never got divorced, and my father never moved out of the house, but he wasn't around much, he didn't pay much attention to me, and I always missed him. I still miss him." You can also reveal your past fears: "When I started high school I was terrified I wouldn't be popular with the other kids."

Writing Your Own Story

It could be very therapeutic for you and your child to write the story of your lives, remembering the best from the past, sifting through family pictures and recalling good times together. If you do write your history, include all the good things to come, and make it turn out the way you want. And then start working at creating those positive memories for the future. You have the power and the opportunity to do things together now that you will remember with joy 10 or 20 years from now. Start now and make it a habit. Do something together this week that you will recall with a smile for years to come.

TEN COMMANDMENTS FOR BUILDING YOUR CHILD'S SELF-ESTEEM

Self-esteem plays a central role in childhood depression. Children with high self-esteem take responsibility for their behavior, make independent decisions, embrace new challenges enthusiastically, tolerate frustration well, show pride in their accomplishments, and manifest a broad range of emotions.

In contrast, children with low self-esteem minimize their own abilities, lack a sense of competence, feel powerless and get frustrated easily, blame others for their problems, avoid taking risks, are easily influenced by others, and exhibit constricted emotions.

Here are 10 ways you can boost your child's self-esteem:

1. Respect your child. Value his feelings, his dignity, and his privacy. Explaining your expectations shows respect for your child. When children don't know what's expected of them, they feel awkward, confused, and fearful. For them to feel comfortable and to be successful in a situation, they need to know ahead of time what to expect.

2. Avoid embarrassing your child. At times you may even need to protect her from embarrassing herself, especially in front of her peers. Embarrassment destroys self-esteem and self-confidence.

3. Show interest in your child. Ask about his thoughts and feelings, his games and friends, his hopes and fears. Your sincere interest reminds him that he is important and worthwhile.

4. Create situations in which your child can be a success. She can succeed at school by being diligent and patient. She might excel at sports with effort and enthusiasm. A child can express creativity and uniqueness through the arts. She can also succeed in

relationships by giving and receiving affection. Encourage any kind of competence.

5. Acknowledge your child's efforts as well as his achievements. Effort matters even when a success is not complete. In fact, you'll have to spend a lot of time encouraging and rewarding effort before you'll ever see a tangible achievement. Acknowledge what is positive about your child's effort, while avoiding criticism of the negative.

Some people are so self-conscious about their performance that they can't tolerate even positive feedback without becoming anxious. Your child may be overly focused on pleasing people, especially you. If so, when you admire his work, try describing it rather than evaluating it.

6. Point out your child's increasing skills. Say, "Look at how you've improved your handwriting from last year to this," or "You really took good care of your little brothers this afternoon. I think you're ready to babysit by yourself now." It's vital to a child's self-esteem to know that she's not only lovable but capable, and that her capability is increasing. When you describe a child's work, she can see the improvement for herself rather than just relying on your evaluation of it.

7. Keep your expectations reasonable and match them to your child. Expectations evoke energy and excitement when you and your child share them, but they can cause confusion and anxiety when they remain hidden or unclear.

8. Accept all your child's feelings. When your child has to do something he dislikes, for example, acknowledge his feelings by saying something like, "I know you don't want to do the dishes, but tonight's your night." Support your child's self-esteem by recognizing and accepting his real feelings.

Since boredom depresses self-esteem while excitement increases it, you can try to help your child find a creative way to accomplish tasks he dislikes. You needn't deny the boring and frustrating aspects of life, but you *can* try to help your child find imaginative ways of coping with the inevitable tedium.

9. Find ways for your child to be helpful to you. It shows you trust and value her. A child's self-esteem grows when she feels genuinely capable of helping you.

10. Give your children the freedom, the responsibility, and the control to make choices. Let them take the lead sometimes.

9

THERAPY FOR YOUR DEPRESSED CHILD

By now, you've already brought your depressed child to his doctor, who has ruled out or treated any of the physical problems that can mimic depression (see Chapter 3). The doctor may have suggested psychotherapy or antidepressant medication, or perhaps you've independently come to the conclusion that your depressed child could benefit from such treatment.

The treatment of a depressed child usually involves several modalities, from talking or play therapy to medication, from individual sessions to multifamily groups. Your child may need one or several of these interventions and you should know what each entails. In order to select the very best therapist for your child, you also need to learn which professionals are qualified to do which kinds of therapy.

In addition to discussing how to find a suitable psychotherapist for your child and exploring the various types of therapy, this chapter will highlight the many ways you can help reinforce and practice the skills your child will be learning in her therapy sessions.

WHO DOES CHILD THERAPY?

Professional Credentials

The therapist you choose for your child may be a psychiatrist, a psychologist, a social worker, or a master's-level counselor. While a therapist's academic background matters less than his skill in working effectively with depressed children, investigating a therapist's credentials can assure you of a certain level of expertise.

CHILD PSYCHIATRISTS are medical doctors who have completed four years of medical school, a one-year internship, two to three years of residency training in adult psychiatry, and two or more years of training in child and adolescent psychiatry. Because they have medical training, psychiatrists are licensed and qualified to prescribe medications for their patients.

CHILD PSYCHOLOGISTS have undergone about five years of graduate training, including a year of internship working with children and several half-year programs of supervised clinical experience. In addition, many states require psychologists to do postdoctoral clinical work before they can be licensed.

SOCIAL WORKERS complete a two-year graduate program consisting of classes and fieldwork. Some states require social workers to accumulate several years of postgraduate clinical experience in order to qualify for licensing.

OTHER MENTAL HEALTH PROFESSIONALS may be equipped to do therapy with your depressed child as well. Some master's-level psychologists or counselors, for example, have completed clinical internships that prepare them to do child therapy.

Which Practitioner Does What Kind of Therapy?

Differences in theoretical approach and even in training tend to carry less weight than differences in the therapists' personalities. Research has shown, in fact, that successful therapists all tend to behave in similar ways. So don't be discouraged if you can't get a prospective therapist to commit to an exclusive approach. Most good therapists will use whatever works. But this is not the same thing as saying that anyone can do child therapy.

What Makes a Good Child Therapist?

At the very least, your child's therapist needs a basic under-standing of normal and abnormal child development and of family dynamics. This provides the foundation for the necessary training in the diagnosis and treatment of clini-cal disorders in children and adolescents. A child therapist should also be committed to the welfare of the children and adolescents in her care. At times this requires active sup-port, while at other times the therapist will need to actively confront a child or define the limits of acceptable behavior. Sometimes a child therapist must advocate for the child with parents, school, or other agencies; at other times, it is most important to listen empathetically and be patient.

A good therapist respects each child's thoughts and feel-ings, and can tolerate a wide range of emotions and im-pulses. She should tell both parents and children exactly what can be kept confidential and what can't, and she should make no promises she can't keep.

A child therapist must deal honestly with her patients, explaining what will happen in therapy and how therapy works. I usually tell the child something like, "We'll be meeting once a week for the next couple of months to talk about the things that have been bothering you. We'll put our heads together to try to understand your problems and see if we can find some ways for you to feel better." We then go on to talk about what therapy involves, depending on the child's particular concerns and developmental level.

Like all human beings, child therapists possess a mixture of needs, such as a need to be liked, to be in control, to be right, or to succeed. Just like a good parent, however, a good therapist must recognize and rein in his own needs to avoid using his patients to meet them or to correct shortcomings in his own childhood.

Your child's therapist should be comfortable with his own life and manifest considerable self-understanding and self-control. These qualities will probably be difficult for you to assess when first meeting a potential therapist. But you can certainly get an impression about a child therapist from a telephone conversation and a face-to-face interview (see below).

Ultimately, it's the relationship between your child and her therapist that will lead to positive changes in your child. If you've ever wondered why a child does well one year in school and poorly the next, one possibility is the difference in her relationship with the two different teachers. Within the therapeutic relationship, your child will learn to experience herself and her world differently. It pays to do a bit of research to find a person with whom your depressed child can develop this therapeutic relationship.

Unfortunately, in many states, anyone can simply award himself the title "psychotherapist" or "counselor," hang out a shingle, and charge a fee to unsuspecting clients. That's why you can't simply pick a "child therapist" out of the Yellow Pages.

CHOOSING YOUR CHILD'S THERAPIST

First of all, take a look at your health insurance policy to see what, if any, mental health benefits it covers. Note, for example, whether outpatient expenses (such as therapy) as well as inpatient expenses (for hospitalization) are reimbursed. Learn exactly what percentage of your child's therapy may be covered, note whether a deductible applies, and determine the maximum yearly payment.

You should also find out whether your insurance company will make so-called third-party payments to any provider you choose, or whether your choices are limited. In some states, for example, third-party payments from insurance and Medicaid can go only to medical doctors. In one of these states, you would be limited to choosing a child psychiatrist. Elsewhere, alternative providers, such as psychologists, social workers, or family counselors, may be reimbursed, especially if they are supervised by a psychiatrist. Determine exactly how much your insurance will pay for your child's therapy, for how long, and who is eligible to receive such payment.

If you belong to a health maintenance organization (HMO), your mental health benefits may be limited to short-term therapy with a social worker or psychologist, with an occasional referral to a staff psychiatrist. Members of preferred provider organizations (PPOs) will probably be limited to a list of mental health providers who agree to accept the reimbursement provisions of the PPO.

Since many insurance policies and health care plans cover mental health treatment inadequately, you may have to pay for your child's therapy out of your own pocket. But you needn't despair. Most clinics and some private practitioners operate on a sliding fee scale basis, charging only what a patient can afford. You might check with a local mental health center to get an estimate of where your family income puts you on their sliding scale.

Private Practitioner or Clinic?

After you have assessed your insurance coverage and your financial situation, consider whether to seek out a private practitioner or a clinic. Particularly in rural areas, a family service agency or mental health center may be your only choice.

Not surprisingly, treatment in a clinic will usually prove less expensive than that provided by a private practitioner. However, since waiting lists may present a one- to six-month delay, you may not be able to get your child into treatment for a considerable time. In most clinics, you won't get to choose your child's therapist, but must accept the next available practitioner. Your child may be treated by a supervised therapist-in-training, whose internship may not last as long as your child needs to be in therapy.

Though it usually costs more, choosing a private therapist may give you more leeway to find a person you and your child can feel compatible with. Often, though not always, a private therapist can give you a fair guarantee that he will be available for as long as your child needs to be in therapy.

Fees

Fees depend on the treatment setting, the region of the country, and on the education and credentials of the practitioner. Private therapists usually charge a fee based on the amount of time spent with the patient. A family therapy session usually lasts longer than an individual session and is proportionally more expensive. Group therapy, lasting about an hour and a half, is usually less expensive than individual treatment. Child psychiatrists and therapists spend a considerable amount of time outside of sessions conferring with teachers, parents, and others involved in the care of the child, so charges will be applied for this work.

Making a List of Candidates

If your insurance will pay for your choice of provider or if money poses no problem, begin by making a list of the criteria you feel are most important in a therapist. You may, for example, prefer a therapist of a particular age or gender, professional background, philosophic viewpoint, or type of experience. After determining what's most important to you, ask a wide variety of sources for the names of possible therapists who meet your personal criteria.

You might ask your family doctor, friends, neighbors, coworkers, relatives, clergy, and involved personnel at your child's school for the names of qualified mental health professionals whom they think might work effectively with your child. If your friends have had children in therapy, ask about their experiences with particular therapists. If you know people involved in mental health professions, ask for their impressions of practitioners with whom they've worked. Be sure to describe your child's needs and be sure to consider any potential therapist's experience with similar children.

You might also call local professional societies for referrals to social workers, psychologists, or psychiatrists. You should be aware, though, that the referrals you'll get from these sources will not be based on knowledge of you or your child, nor will they reflect the excellence of a particular practitioner. Instead, referrals like this are usually made on a strict rotating basis.

Now that you have compiled a list of names, try rank ordering them. Put the names you've heard from several people at the top of your list.

Telephone Interviews

You'll probably be able to narrow your list by talking to several therapists on the phone. Start at the top of your list. Ask the practitioners you speak to whether they treat depressed children, what their fee is, whether they will reduce it if you can't afford it, and whether they have any time available to treat your child. You may want to set up appointments with two or three different therapists to see which one you like best.

Depending on the therapist's training, your child's age, your family's makeup, and the nature of the problem, a potential therapist may want to meet first with you, with your child alone, or with your whole family at once.

I usually meet first with the parents of a younger child. That way I can learn more about the child's problem, development, and general functioning, and about the family's medical concerns.

When the patient is an adolescent, I usually meet with her first in order to convey respect for her views and to show the importance I place on her active involvement. From speaking to a parent or school counselor on the phone, I usually have enough of an idea of the problem to help me guide the conversation if the teenager is reticent.

Meeting with a Potential Therapist

You will probably spend most of the first appointment discussing your child's history and the problems that brought him to therapy. Make sure you save some time at the end to ask the therapist some of the following questions:

- What is your training?
- Where were you trained?
- Are you licensed/certified as a therapist in this state?
- How much training and experience have you had working with depressed children?
- What kind of treatment do you think will help my child?
- How will my spouse and I be involved in the treatment?
- How often will you see my child?
- Do you have any idea how long the therapy might take?

- Are you eligible to collect third-party payments?
- Will insurance or Medicaid cover all or part of your fee?
- What arrangements do you make for canceled appointments?
- How soon can we expect an improvement in our child?
- How will we know if the therapy is working?

After you meet with an individual practitioner, you can get a fair idea of whether you and your child will be able to work with this person by pondering some of these questions: Did the therapist pay careful attention to what you had to say? Do you think she understood your child's problems? Were her explanations or suggestions clear and reasonable? Did she seem willing to talk openly about practical details, such as emergency phone arrangements and arrangements for missed appointments? Did she treat you with respect and courtesy? Did her treatment plan make sense to you?

Although this may not happen until the second or third meeting, setting goals for treatment should come early in therapy and should involve you, your child, and the therapist. If the problems are where you're starting from, the goals are where you're going. Together they determine the best route to get there and a map to tell whether you're on the right track.

For example, if your child feels sad every day, has no friends, and regularly tries to stay home from school, your initial goals may be to get him to the point where he feels happy 80 percent of the time, makes three new friends, and willingly goes to school every day. At the end of one month you can easily assess how many sad days he has compared to happy ones, what progress he's made toward making friends, and how often he resists going to school. That way you'll have some indication of whether or not your child is making progress.

Choosing a Therapist for a Depressed Adolescent

Just as the developmental tasks of the adolescent differ from those of a younger child, so do her therapeutic needs. In a teenager, depression arises in the midst of developmental issues such as the need to establish independence from parents and the task of coping with increased sexual and aggressive drives.

Therapists who work well with adolescents may differ temperamentally from those who prefer to deal with children or adults. Working with adolescents certainly requires a sense of humor and relative comfort with your personal flaws, because adolescents will remind you of them time and again. A therapist needs to relax with teenagers and show them how to be comfortable with who they are.

On the other hand, the therapist should not try to be their buddy or to relate to them as a peer. Like a parent, a therapist carries a lot of responsibility and must take that seriously. Both group and individual therapy allow room for some fun, but the therapist needs to set the limits.

An adolescent should be as fully involved as she wants to be in selecting her therapist, and she should have the right not to work with someone she doesn't feel comfortable with. But if your adolescent is so depressed and withdrawn that she just doesn't seem to care, or so irritable that she rejects every therapist, you will have to make the choice for her. Teenagers should certainly be taking on many responsibilities for themselves, but a depressed child or adolescent needs therapy whether she thinks she needs it or not. It's your job to make sure she gets it.

Since an adolescent tends to want more of the therapist to herself than does a younger child, I usually split the family and individual therapy of an adolescent between two different therapists. For the good of the adolescent and her family, parents need to be kept informed, but I usually do that in periodic reviews with the adolescent and her family together. During the course of therapy, I solicit information from parents and school personnel to help me understand an adolescent's current situation and plan her treatment accordingly.

WHAT GOES ON IN THERAPY AND HOW YOU CAN HELP AT HOME

Psychotherapists usually concentrate on one of the following approaches with depressed children: psychodynamic therapy, cognitive-behavioral therapy, or family therapy. A therapist's orientation will affect the types of intervention he advises, how many sessions a week he offers, and how long the therapy will eventually last. Though many therapists currently draw techniques and principles from several schools, and though any type of therapy can be combined with medication or group therapy, most therapists subscribe to one of these three basic methods.

- Psychodynamic therapy: Psychodynamic theory holds that symptoms arise because of internal emotional conflicts. The main therapeutic focus is to identify these conflicts, gain insight into how they arose, and ultimately reach a healthier compromise with the self. Based on the theories of Sigmund Freud and his followers, psychodynamic therapy concentrates on helping children look inward. A child who is too young to talk may be encouraged to show his feelings through play. Psychodynamic therapy aims to help a child understand and resolve the conflicts in his life. Because gaining such insight often takes considerable time, psychodynamic therapists may recommend therapeutic sessions several times each week over a period of several years.
- Cognitive-behavioral therapy: With its roots in experimental psychology, cognitive-behavioral therapy

trains a child to think about the world and himself differently and to alter troubling behavioral patterns without necessarily pursuing insight into the origins of such behavior. This type of therapy tends to be short-term, typically lasting for months rather than years.

- Family therapy: Family therapists see the depressed child as "the identified patient" within a troubled family, and meet with the whole family in order to modify the maladaptive behaviors of all its members. Family therapy might last anywhere from a session or two to over a year.

Your child's therapy may well include several aspects of these therapies, described in greater detail below. You certainly shouldn't become your child's cotherapist, but your efforts to back up these programs will multiply their therapeutic benefits.

Psychodynamic Therapy

TALKING THERAPY Psychodynamic therapy focuses on helping a child understand himself and his feelings. Examining memories and dreams may yield valuable clues about unconscious ideas that have influenced the child's current state of mind.

For example, a child may become inconsolably upset about the death of a pet. Psychotherapy can help the child discover that deep inside he is also remembering his father's disappearance when his parents separated for six months, or re-experiencing the unavailability of his mother years earlier when she was depressed and preoccupied. In casting light on these hidden themes, psychodynamic therapy can help a child understand how past events might be aggravating his reaction to today's events.

Jocelyn, 15, was in psychotherapy for depression. One day she opened our session by saying, "Last night I dreamed I was with my friends at a beach, and I found a buried treasure. It was a treasure chest and my brother helped me dig it out of the sand. No one else believed it was down there, but it was, and it had beautiful shells and things in it."

Jocelyn and I talked in the session about the meaning of the dream, and together we decided that it had to do with the good and beautiful things inside Jocelyn, the treasures that no one believes are there. The digging and uncovering she thought was like our therapy sessions, where we look for things about her that are buried, and she thought I was like her brother in the dream, helping her and believing in her.

Another time Jocelyn reported a dream in which she was driving a racing car: "I was driving a red Ferrari, I guess it was my mother's, and it was fun to be driving it, but I couldn't control the speed. It kept going faster and faster, and as I was speeding along these streets there was a cop at every corner with his ticket book, scowling at me, but I never did get a ticket. It was a little scary, and I was worried because it was my mother's car, but it was fun, too."

This dream proved to be so rich in imagery that we came back to it several times. Jocelyn decided that racing the Ferrari represented several dangerous but tempting activities: drinking, drugs, and sex. The fact that it was her mother's car probably had to with some envy of her mother's sophisticated allure. At first Jocelyn thought the cop was her father, but months later, as she recognized her own strict conscience, Jocelyn began to think of the cop as just another side of herself.

Psychodynamic therapy also pays close attention to intrapsychic defense mechanisms such as denial. The mind employs denial to shield itself from painful awareness, but denial itself can aggravate matters. Until a teenager faces up to his drinking problem, for example, he will not be able to work on his depression.

All good therapists, but particularly psychodynamic therapists, cultivate a sensitivity to such resistance. They understand that individuals, and families too, often resist change, even when they are suffering. Therapists have to be prepared to deal with resistance—canceled or missed appointments or empty talk that avoids the real subject—whenever it arises, or else the therapy will fail.

Psychodynamic therapy frequently mixes supportive elements along with insight. The supportive aspects of the therapy include the therapist's efforts to reassure and encourage the child. The therapist might share advice about problems the child is facing and perhaps suggest alternative strategies to try in different situations.

PLAY THERAPY A depressed child often suffers silently with worries and conflicts that she can't comfortably express to anyone. Play therapy has proven particularly useful for dealing with these internal aspects of depression. This form of therapy also benefits younger children who can't yet readily put their thoughts and feelings into words.

The therapist provides different activities depending on the child's maturity, preferences, and mood. Children may progress from free play to drawing to board games to conversation. Such play can serve as a channel for expressing both inner concerns—for example, the fear that a parent might disappear—and real-life events, such as instances of humiliation or neglect.

Therapists usually schedule play sessions once or twice a week for 30 to 40 minutes. The therapist sometimes watches the play and sometimes joins in, periodically offering comments to help the child understand herself and her difficulties. At times he may suggest the child solve problems by playing things out another way.

For example, Jonathan's father died suddenly when the boy was 4. Now 5, Jonathan was suffering a depression marked by deep sadness and difficulty falling asleep.

The boy never said much about his father's death and had cried only once. Jonathan's mother assumed his father's death "didn't really affect him" because his father had worked so much that he hadn't had a lot of contact with the boy.

In play therapy, Jonathan usually chose to play with the doll family and their house. He always chose two child dolls and a mother, and he played out a variety of situations, but he never went beyond evening time. Instead, Jonathan would always skip to the next morning. After a couple of months, when considerable trust and warmth had developed between the boy and his therapist, Jonathan was playing with the dolls "after dinner" and his therapist decided to explore the bedtime issue.

"When will it be time for the children to go to bed?" the therapist asked.

"They can't go to bed," Jonathan replied.

"Why not?"

"They don't have a Daddy."

"They can't go to bed without a Daddy?"

"No, because he always reads them stories before bed and they can't sleep without a story." And the little boy's brown eyes filled with tears.

Over the next several sessions, Jonathan played out bedtime scenes over and over, sometimes having the therapist use the Daddy doll. Then, at the therapist's suggestion, Jonathan had the Mommy doll read stories.

In collateral sessions with Jonathan's mother, the therapist helped her to see how sad Jonathan actually felt about his father's death. The mother also got the chance to work through some of the unresolved grief that had made it hard for her to fill in for her deceased husband. Jonathan's play became progressively more joyful, and, as his mother grew stronger, she began to appear in his play more often. Within a year Jonathan was doing very well and sleeping soundly through the night.

What You Can Do   Most children use play as therapy for themselves long before they ever see a therapist. After all, play presents an opportunity to reshape the world and relationships. When he plays, your child can correct things to make them come out the way he wishes. For your child, play is repair as well as practice, experimentation as well as escape.

In order to play with your children, you'll have to be there, make time, and join them in a different world with different rules. In fact, you may find yourself following their rules for the first time.

Maybe you'll have to be the baby, for example, and your child will get to be the parent. You might have to sit on the floor or crawl into a fort made out of cushions from the sofa. You might have to do ridiculous things like popping out from under a blanket 20 straight times and pretend you're really surprised again each time. Maybe you'll be a tiger and crawl all around the house looking for tiger food.

War, house, school, dolls: the choices are endless. But when you play with your child you'll be spending time with her, and you'll probably learn much more about her than you ever could just by sitting her down and asking her how she's feeling or what she's worried about.

So make time to play with your child. Try to forget about work and all your other responsibilities for a while. Unplug the phone if you have to. But find half an hour to play and open yourself up to your child and the experience.

Let your child choose from a wide variety of materials that encourage imaginative play: blocks, dolls and figures, paper and crayons, clay, for example. Make sure you have a place to play where you're not worried about making a mess. Older children also like to draw. Some may want to write a story or poem, or dictate one to you. Don't worry about grammar and punctuation; this is playing, after all.

Playing catch or kicking a soccer ball around is a more active way to play with your kids. Sports can be a good means to teach them how to handle competition as well as winning and losing. Taking a walk or a bike ride is another wonderful way to spend time with your children.

As you play and spend time with your children, you can listen to what they say, watch what they do, and be aware of the themes that seem to interest them. Note the feelings they express even if they attribute those feelings to a doll or another character. Don't worry about what to reply. Simply go with the flow and keep an open mind and an open heart. You don't have to *try* to be therapeutic to be therapeutic.

Learning-Oriented Therapy

Therapy that attempts to teach your child new skills will probably include elements of cognitive therapy, unlearning helplessness, social skills training, and problem-solving.

COGNITIVE THERAPY   The techniques of cognitive therapy can help your child identify, examine, and modify distorted thinking as well as dysfunctional beliefs, such as "I'm no good at all." In therapy your child will learn to recognize the connections between his thoughts, his emotions, and his behavior. He'll get practice monitoring his negative thoughts by examining the rational evidence for and against them. Finally, he'll be trained to substitute realistic interpretations for distorted thoughts and feelings.

According to cognitive theory, people feel depressed because of errors in their thinking. These errors include arbitrary inference, selective perception, personalization, magnification, black or white thinking, and overgeneralization.

- *Arbitrary (negative) inference* means interpreting an event in a negative way, without knowing the truth of the matter, and in spite of the fact that an alternative explanation exists. For example, when your child's friend doesn't call her one night, she might jump to the conclusion that her friend doesn't like her anymore. But it could well be that her friend was busy at an activity and didn't get home until late, or that she didn't feel well, or that she had too much homework and didn't have time to talk on the phone, or that she misbehaved and her parents forbade her to use the phone.

- *Selective perception* involves picking out the negative aspects of a situation and focusing on them to the exclusion of the positive. For example, perhaps your teenager goes to his first dance and everything goes fine except that he knocks over a glass of punch. The next day all your son can think about is how he ruined the evening by being so clumsy and that the girl he was with probably thinks he's an idiot.

- *Personalization* refers to the error of perceiving external negative events as one's own fault. Your child, for example, may blame herself for your divorce.

- *Magnification* means taking a small problem and blowing it out of proportion. For example, your son may break down in tears in the car as you drop him off for school because he forgot the baseball cards he was going to show to a friend. He imagines his friend will be uncontrollably angry or inconsolably disappointed and won't even want to talk to him. Your son's day is ruined.

  Minimization of positive events is the opposite distortion. When your daughter gets an A on her social studies test, she may dismiss your congratulations with, "It was an easy test because it only covered half a chapter and it doesn't count for very much."

- *Black-or-white thinking* makes a child believe that if he makes a mistake he's a complete failure; if he doesn't understand a new math concept he's "totally stupid"; if he strikes out once, he "never was any good at sports."

- *Overgeneralization* refers to the error of assuming that one specific difficulty proves a major pattern of problems. Your child thinks, "I can't spell p-o-t-a-t-o,

I'm a terrible speller," or "I wasn't invited to Susan's party because everyone hates me."

Cognitive therapy aims to improve a child's mood by correcting these errors in thinking. Cognitive treatment of depression usually takes three to four months of weekly sessions in which the troublesome automatic thoughts are discussed, and rational explanations developed to replace the cognitive distortions.

Homework may include rehearsing difficult situations in the imagination and thinking of alternative solutions, or discovering activities that improve the mood and spending more time at these. In addition, patients frequently keep a journal of their activities, thoughts, and feelings between sessions.

What You Can Do   You might start by helping your child make a mood-activity journal. In it, she can keep a daily record of her different activities, rating her mood from very sad (1) to very happy (5). Then, after reviewing the journal together to identify the activities that make her happiest, encourage her to spend more time that way.

Once your child is able to record what she's doing (activity) and what she's feeling (mood) on a regular basis, she might want to add a column for what she's thinking. Then together you can begin to identify the negative thoughts that go along with her sad feelings.

For example, Sheila, 12, had a lot of difficulty on school mornings. She was extremely slow at getting up and needed constant reminders from her mother. Naturally, this escalated tensions between them. In therapy Sheila and her mother analyzed the problem. After discussing the pattern in detail, Sheila identified her feelings as nervousness and dread when she awakened every morning.

Sheila and her mother made a chart. They included what she was doing (getting dressed and ready for school) in one column and what she was feeling (nervousness,

dread) in another. Then they made a column for what
Sheila was thinking.

Over a period of a week, as Sheila began to notice her
own "automatic" thoughts in the morning, she realized she
was thinking things like: "I'll probably get called on in
class and not know the answer and make a fool of myself,"
or "No one will want to sit with me at lunch."

After you've identified the negative thoughts that your
child thinks on a regular basis, try to evaluate them together in order to decide whether they are rational or
distorted. Sheila and her mother talked about her automatic negative thoughts. Her mother reminded the girl
that she had received C's and B's on her last report card,
and asked, "What percentage of correct answers on tests
and assignments does it take to get a B?"

"Between eighty and ninety percent, I guess."

"How about a C?"

"Seventy to eighty percent."

"So you actually knew the answers to at least seventy and
sometimes ninety percent of the questions?"

"Yeah, I guess so."

"So more often than not, actually the majority of the
time, you'll know the answer to the question."

"Yeah, but I get nervous standing up and answering in
front of the whole class."

Then you can begin to substitute a more rational
thought for the distorted negative one that has been contributing to your child's depression:

"Maybe part of the reason for being nervous is that you
think you're going to get the answer wrong."

"Yeah, I know it is, that's what I'm saying to myself the
whole time: 'I'm not gonna know this, I'm gonna get this
wrong, I'm gonna feel like a fool.' "

"That would make it hard to answer correctly even if you
knew the answer! Why don't you try talking to yourself a
different way . . ."

"Like how?"

"Like say, 'I did my homework last night and I know this stuff pretty well. I can answer most questions right.' "

"I could try that, but I would secretly sort of doubt it, I think."

"That's all right. Just start talking to yourself that way. We both know it's true, and after a while, you'll believe it, too."

Another useful technique you can use at home is the "pros and cons" technique. Like cognitive therapy, this technique comes from the work of Dr. Aaron Beck and his colleagues at the University of Pennsylvania.

Sheila admitted that sometimes she would fake a headache or stomachache so that she wouldn't have to go to school. Like many depressed children, however, Sheila had considered only one side of the issue. When she and her mother sat down and made a list of the pros and cons of staying home "sick" from school, Sheila gained a more balanced perspective.

Pros:

Won't have to stand up and answer in front of class.
Won't feel nervousness.
Won't feel stupid.
Won't have to worry about who will sit with me at lunch.

Cons:

Will feel guilty about staying home.
Will miss lessons and class notes, getting further behind and feeling more nervous.
Can't spend time with my friends.
My parents will be upset.
Makes it harder to go back to school and face kids the next day.

Sheila taped her list to her nightstand and every morning when she woke up she looked at it to remind herself that in the long run staying home was worse than going to school.

UNLEARNING HELPLESSNESS   You may recall from Chapter 3 that childhood depression can represent a kind of learned helplessness. Indeed, while normal children ascribe failure to insufficient effort on their part, depressed children tend to attribute failure and helplessness to an innate lack of ability. Your child's therapist will retrain him to realize that when a task is appropriate, failure usually stems from insufficient effort. With his therapist's encouragement, your child will learn the rewards of persistence.

For example, Alexis, 11, came to her therapy session in tears because she could not do a math homework problem. She threw down her book angrily, shouting, "I can't get it, I'm too dumb." I said, "I know you're not dumb from the way you figured out how to get that door lock unstuck for me," mentioning a specific problem I had watched her solve just that afternoon.

Being careful not to criticize Alexis for not trying hard enough or being lazy, I suggested she and I go back to review the sample problems earlier in the chapter of her math book. What's therapeutic about this intervention is the combination of encouragement with an active problem-solving strategy. You, of course, can easily do the same thing for your child.

What You Can Do   Teach your children that they have a considerable amount of control over their lives, and that success comes from effort and perseverance, not just luck. For example, when your daughter accomplishes something such as getting a good grade or learning a new athletic skill, congratulate her by pointing out to her how her efforts paid off: "That was terrific when you scored the winning goal. All your practice in the backyard really paid off."

If your child doesn't achieve a realistic goal he set for himself, talk about how he could try again with a little more effort: "You must have been disappointed with that C minus in history. I guess you'll need to make it more of a priority for study this next quarter. I learned some tricks for memorizing names and dates from one of my high school history teachers, and if you want I'll show you."

You probably already know that you are an important role model for your child. When you achieve a success yourself, demonstrate pride in your own accomplishments and mention how hard you worked for them: "It really felt good to hear so many positive remarks about my presentation. I spent a lot of time and effort making sure it would be good." By the same token, when you have a disappointment, admit it and speculate on what you might do better next time. "I was upset with myself for not golfing better today. But I'll have to spend a lot more time on the driving range if I expect to break ninety."

SOCIAL SKILLS TRAINING Some learning theorists believe that children become depressed when they get too little positive reinforcement from others, perhaps because they lack certain basic social skills.

Indeed, depressed children do seem to be unable to start a light conversation, to make a joke or to laugh at someone else's joke, to look people in the eye and smile, to respond to a compliment, or to act confident and positive. In short, they can't do the very things that would make other children want to play with them and get to know them better.

Of course, this problem feeds upon itself. A child with inadequate social skills has trouble getting along with others and he may be excluded from a variety of social activities. Indeed, as long as your depressed child can't make friends, her feelings of loneliness and inadequacy will only grow.

Social skills training seeks to teach depressed children the verbal and nonverbal behaviors they need to get along with other people. Through instruction, group discussion, therapist modeling, and role-playing—even videotaping and replaying—depressed children can learn how to do all these things: read social cues, recognize other people's feelings and needs, have a social conversation, make new friends, and deal with conflicts. Through practice in and out of therapy, your child will acquire new social skills and experience progressively more social "rewards" in the form of acceptance by peers, more and better friendships, and a sense of interpersonal competence.

What You Can Do   Social skills are basically people skills, the things you do without even thinking about them to connect with other people and get a relationship going. Social skills comprise everything from small talk about sports or the weather to a sincere sharing of important feelings. While athletic skills help you play a sport well and intellectual skills help you learn, social skills help you get along well with other people.

Whether you know it or not, you've acquired many social skills through the years. For example, you know the importance of looking someone in the eye when you're talking to him, of offering your hand in greeting, of not interrupting someone who's talking, and of smiling to show your friendliness. You can teach your own child many of the useful social skills you possess.

Model healthy social skills in your interactions with your children and others. Show them the respect of saying please and thank you, and of listening attentively when they speak no matter how young they are. Say hello and goodbye, good morning and good night. It's all too easy to get lazy and take a person's presence for granted when you live with him day in and day out, but don't. Acknowledge your child's presence and show him you're happy to see him.

Do things as a family that provide an opportunity to teach and exercise social skills. For example, go out to dinner and practice good manners. Visit a friend's home and be a considerate guest. Talk to your children before you go about what's involved and give them credit for acting appropriately. (You know, of course, that social skills involve a little acting.)

Since social skills go way beyond saying please and thank you, you may find it helpful to role-play certain situations. You want your child to learn tactics for starting a conversation with someone she doesn't know, of giving and accepting compliments, of tactfully declining an invitation she doesn't want to accept, of asking for help, of dealing with peer pressure, of standing up for a friend, of expressing negative feelings, and of responding effectively to teasing.

You know your child won't learn these things in the school curriculum, and you also know that successful strategies can be hard for kids to figure out by themselves. But you've been through many of these situations yourself, so you have a lot of wisdom and experience to offer your child.

You can probably anticipate common tough situations, and simply deal with others as they come along. Role-play with your depressed child to find a style and solution he can be comfortable with.

You could even make up scenarios to talk about and decide what to do in certain situations, such as the following:

- You notice a new student sitting alone at lunchtime and looking upset.
- You introduce yourself to someone on your soccer team and she turns around and looks the other way.
- You'd like to get involved in the class play but you've never done it before.
- You are upset when a group of your classmates make fun of your new haircut.
- Your feelings get hurt when you're not invited to a party.

PROBLEM-SOLVING SKILLS TRAINING Faced with problems, depressed children tend to think of fewer alternative solutions. They also fail to read other people's feelings accurately or understand what causes people's behavior. Depressed children frequently underestimate the consequences of their own behavior and they may focus more on end results (usually seen in all-or-nothing terms) than on the intermediate steps and the process of reaching a goal.

In therapy, problem-solving skills training will teach your child how to solve interpersonal problems in a step-by-step fashion using demonstrations, structured exercises, role-playing, and real-life stories.

What You Can Do You can model and teach effective problem-solving skills for your children every day. Not every problem can be solved, but almost every problem can be managed if you take the following five logical steps:

1. *Define the problem.* When you sense a problem because you feel upset or because someone else believes there's a problem, figure out as exactly as possible what the problem is and whose problem it is. Get the facts.
2. *Identify your goal.* Figure out what you want to accomplish by solving the problem...to forget about it? to get your old friend back? to earn a higher grade? to get along better with your parents?
3. *Brainstorm.* Think of all the possible things you could do to solve the problem, even seemingly impossible or ridiculous solutions. This is the time to make a list and don't leave anything off. The more alternatives the better. Think creatively. Refuse to settle for either-or thinking.
4. *Weigh the pros and cons.* Evaluate all the possibilities, comparing the probable consequences, the effects on other people, the likelihood of accomplishing your goal, the risks, the moral acceptability. Choose the best alternative.

5. *Take action.* Do it. Try it. Put your plan into action and see what happens. Use feedback to modify your behavior the next time. In other words, learn from your mistakes as well as your successes.

Family Therapy

A specialized approach to problems like childhood depression, family therapy involves the entire family. In fact, in family therapy, the depressed individual is termed "the identified patient."

The theory behind family therapy grew out of "general systems theory," which considers the family as a living system. Like any other living system, a family is governed by a set of rules, has identifiable boundaries, and relies on communication between its parts. General systems theorists suggest that causes for an individual's depression can be understood only within the context of the family system. And they describe these causes in circular rather than in linear terms.

For example, instead of concluding that Johnny is depressed because his father is distant and unavailable, a family therapist might describe a recurring series of family interactions that form this circular pattern. When Johnny acts depressed, his father pulls away because he interprets depression as weakness and it reminds him of depressive aspects in himself. When Johnny's father pulls away, his mother becomes anxious and draws closer to Johnny by nursing him through his depression. As his mother becomes more solicitous, Johnny becomes more depressed and needy, which encourages his mother's pampering but provokes his father's further withdrawal. As his father becomes less involved, Johnny becomes even more depressed and seeks even more attention from his mother.

A family therapy technique, circular questioning, grew out of this belief in circular causality. Circular questions explore family patterns by asking one person about the interactions of others, sometimes comparing one to another: "Who gets more upset when you feel too lousy to go to school, John, your mother or your father?" A circular question may explore the past—"If you had gotten depressed before your parents separated, how would they have reacted differently?"—or the future: "When you get over your depression, who will be the next one in the family to get sick?"

Many family therapists believe that symptoms of "the identified patient" actually point up problems within the family system. So, for example, a girl's depression may symbolize everyone else's grief about her father's departure from the family, or distract her parents from their marital conflict, or even serve to help a parent in distress.

In her book, *Sex, Love, and Violence* (W. W. Norton, 1990), Chloe Madanes describes a teenager who attempted suicide, forcing her depressed mother to pull herself together to respond to the immediate crisis. Madanes suggests that the mother was covertly asking her daughter for help, but that the daughter's response, attempted suicide, actually jolted her into competence.

The therapy for this family involved exercises in which the mother "pretended" to be depressed and the daughter helped her in healthier ways such as reassuring her, distracting her, encouraging her with shared activities, and reminding her mother how much she loved her. It worked.

This case illustrates another important family therapy concept, that of family roles. Family therapy frequently focuses on assigning appropriate roles and marking clear boundaries between subsystems like parents and children. In the above case the daughter was asked to temporarily assume the role of parent by taking care of her mother. This therapeutic pretense freed the pair to recover their appropriate roles in real life. Families usually function best when parents have a strong alliance with one another. Then their children can remain children without having to become a substitute, a referee, an ally, or a caretaker for either parent. Therapy with the family of a depressed child tries to address any family issues that may be contributing to a child's depression. In addition, the other family members get help in coping with the stress that affects them all.

Group Therapy

In addition to individual or family therapy, your child may also benefit from group therapy. In group therapy, the group's cohesiveness and interaction take center stage, allowing the leader to serve more as a facilitator than as a therapist. The group might consist of other children or adolescents with similar problems or of families sharing similar concerns. In another type of group situation, networking, all the people who have anything to do with your child may be brought together to seek solutions to his problems.

PEER GROUP THERAPY   Peers become a progressively more powerful element in the lives of children, peaking in importance in early adolescence. Children, especially teenagers, often discuss their problems more freely in such a group than they would in individual therapy.

Jeff, for example, belonged to an "aftercare" group, a therapy group for adolescents who had been previously hospitalized. Several months before, Jeff had attempted suicide. Now back at school and living with his family, the 15-year-old remained depressed about the fact that his girlfriend had broken up with him, and he expressed frustration about his difficulty developing a new relationship.

In the group one day Jeff said, "I saw Cathy in the hall at school today and she was talking to a couple of senior guys and she acted like I didn't even exist."

Another boy in the group who was just as thwarted in his own attempts to establish a relationship with a girl said,

"She's a bitch, man, forget about her. When you see her again just tell her she's a bitch and then ignore her." It made Jeff feel a little better to have someone "on his side," but Dan didn't have much insight into the problem either.

"Aren't you guys being a little unfair to her? Doesn't she have the right to talk to whoever she wants? After all, she isn't going out with you anymore anyway. Why do you care so much? And how do you know she even saw you? How do you know she was intentionally ignoring you?" Karen introduced another perspective by identifying with the girl, and provoking Jeff to look at someone else's feelings.

"Yeah, and didn't you say that she broke up with you after you started paying more attention to some other girl than to her?" Elise has now confronted Jeff and told him he should look at his own behavior, his own role in his problems. Jeff takes this confrontation better from a peer than he might from an adult therapist.

"Well, yeah, I was spending a lot of time with someone else, but it was only because Cathy was getting caught up with her cheerleading and didn't have time for me anyway." Jeff admits some of his own needs and how they weren't being met, but he still doesn't want to take responsibility for his behavior and he blames the girl again.

"Yeah, he's right, cheerleaders are always stuck on themselves anyway." Again Dan wants to see Jeff and himself as victims.

"It seems like both of you guys have had this happen several times with different girls, but you're still not willing to take any of the blame yourselves." Karen is talking again. She uses the unfortunate word *blame*, which gives her message a negative connotation, but she at least continues to insist that both Jeff and Dan take a look at their own behavior. She even points out a recurrent pattern, making it harder for them to deny that they are somehow contributing to the problem.

Such exchanges take place again and again over the weeks of group therapy. The participants get to know each other well. They learn to confront one another's behavior and attitudes openly, while at the same time experiencing a powerful sense of belonging within the group. As depressed teens try new ways of behaving in their own schools and their own lives, they always have the group to return to as a source of acceptance and understanding.

MULTIPLE-FAMILY GROUP THERAPY   This technique may be particularly helpful for the families of adolescents. Like a cross between family therapy and group therapy, multiple-family group therapy involves several families, including parents and adolescents, meeting as a group to discuss common problems. One of my recent multifamily groups featured the following discussion:

Jeanne was talking about her 14-year-old daughter, Clare: "Things between us have changed since she tried to kill herself. I was angry at her and I'm still angry at her for doing something that would have ruined our lives. Her father and I would have been crushed. I don't know how we could have gone on. And now I'm scared all the time, scared that she'll do it again, like if I have to discipline her or make her do something she doesn't like."

"You feel like you're being held hostage," another mother of a suicidal daughter volunteered.

"Exactly," answered Jeanne.

"You act like it's my fault," Clare complained, "like I want to feel this way. I couldn't think of anything else to do. I certainly wasn't going to go to you. You were so mad at me, you didn't want to talk to me."

Both mother and daughter felt angry and afraid, but they could see only their own side of it. Their own overwhelming feelings blinded them to the other's feelings. But one of the other adolescents noticed some similarities with his own situation:

"You have to admit, Clare, that you didn't stop and think what effect it might have on your family if you killed yourself. My father killed himself. It's been two years and I haven't gotten over it at all. I miss him all the time. But I'm kind of angry at him, too, because he didn't think about me and my feelings at the time. He didn't care what he put me through. He could have gotten help."

"I guess you're right. I know it was stupid, but I was so upset at the time."

"On the other hand, I think I know what Clare means," added another mother. "I think I know how you felt, because I've felt that way too. I felt pretty hopeless and I didn't think there was anybody I could turn to. It turns out there were people there for me, just like your mom was probably there for you if she knew, but I didn't know it at the time."

Both Clare and her mother cried. Clare felt that somebody understood what she was feeling, and her mother was relieved that someone recognized that she loved her daughter and that she wasn't a bad mother. The fact that an adult could understand the adolescent, Clare, and an adolescent could see her mother's perspective is an extra benefit of the multiple-family group. People can sometimes hear messages across the generation gap more easily when it comes from someone outside the family. They also seem to listen better to the other group members, perhaps because they're not emotionally involved in the other family's problems.

NETWORKING   Networking may be the ultimate extension of the group approach to therapy. Just as the concept has become popular in the business world as a method of developing relationships that will help you in your career, networking can be used in the treatment of a depressed child or adolescent to create a broad base of support through the crisis of depression and beyond.

Network therapy involves the calling together of a number of people, including but not limited to the immediate family of the depressed child. This group attempts to understand how the problem arose, come up with a plan for correcting it, and follow through as a group with a common purpose.

In discovering or creating a depressed child's support network, I have at times included the following people:

- the immediate family of parents, stepparents, brothers, and sisters
- the extended family of grandparents, uncles, aunts, and cousins
- clergy and church members
- the school community of teachers, principals, school counselors, and coaches
- the peer group of friends and teammates, girlfriends and boyfriends
- police officers
- babysitters
- parents' employers
- the teenager's boss
- any other interested person committed to helping the child and his family

These networks have met in offices, hospitals, schools, and homes. At times we've included people on a conference telephone call from 1,000 miles away. In network therapy, if someone can contribute something to solving the problem, she needs to be involved in the network.

Dave was a 17-year-old high school junior whose school social worker, Julie Woodward, called me because Dave had threatened to "get drunk, go out on my four-wheeler, and kill myself." Cathy Allen, his therapist, had wanted to hospitalize him, but Dave and his father refused. Dave said if he were locked up he would definitely kill himself because he couldn't stand to lose his freedom.

I suggested to Julie and Cathy that they help Dave and his family assemble a network of interested persons and that we would meet and discuss the problem and try to arrive at an alternative solution.

We gathered one night at the therapist's office. The group included Cathy Allen; Julie Woodward; Dave's girlfriend, Anne; his friends, Mark and Joe; Dave's father, Bill; and his mother, Pat.

We began the session by taking everyone's view of the problem. Dave listed his problems as: his parents' divorce, his father's remarriage, and, possibly, a depression. Dave's father thought Dave's problems were an inability to accept the divorce and remarriage, and an unwillingness to take discipline. Pat agreed with Bill's assessment of the problem. She mentioned that she and her ex-husband, Bill, had not talked in four years and she acknowledged that this made things difficult for Dave.

Others in the room added that Dave had problems with his girlfriend, Anne, and that he had a strained relationship with his father. Julie mentioned that Dave had been in fights at school and acted aggressively, both against others and himself. Cathy reminded us that Dave had a court date coming up for breaking another boy's jaw in a fight.

Dave's girlfriend, Anne, felt that Dave's insecurity about their relationship stemmed from the deterioration of his parents' marriage. Joe, a good friend, said he thought Dave's main problem was that he didn't have anyone to talk to. With some coaxing from me, the group agreed that from time to time Dave has a problem with alcohol.

When Dave's friend Mark began to talk about Dave's difficulty talking with his father, it became clear that almost everyone in this system had difficulty talking straight to someone else. Mark and Joe both expressed Dave's feelings toward his father, saying that Dave yearned to be closer with him. Dave and Bill remained silent, but the indirect communication hit its target. When I asked Bill directly if he'd gotten the message, he nodded and said that he did.

When Bill began talking about Dave's problem with his girlfriend, he mentioned an overnight Dave had wanted to go on with Anne and her family and he said he had forbidden it. Bill mentioned that Dave had told him that his mother said he could go. At this point, Pat looked directly at Bill and said in a calm voice that she had never given her permission. Pat and Bill then exchanged a few words about Dave's manipulative behavior. Almost without noticing it, Dave's parents had just accomplished more communication than they had in the previous four years.

The networking session went on to discuss ways in which friends and relatives were willing to work to help Dave. Julie Woodward pointed out that even from the moment Dave heard I had recommended this meeting, his mood and functioning at school had vastly improved. Everyone agreed to continue meeting on a weekly basis for a while to further address Dave's problems. For his part, Dave made a no-suicide promise to his friends and his family.

MEDICATION

You have probably heard about recent advances in treating adult depression with medication. Depressed children, too, can sometimes benefit from these drugs. A child should get medication, however, only as part of a comprehensive treatment plan that also includes therapy.

Depressed children usually receive medication just long enough to treat an acute depressive episode and prevent a relapse. Should your child require antidepressant medication, it will have to be supervised by a medical doctor even if your child continues to see a different mental health professional for psychotherapy.

Because antidepressant medications have potential risks and side effects as well as benefits, ask your child's doctor to carefully explain these as well as the purpose of the medication. You should know, for example, that none of the antidepressants described below has yet been formally approved by the Food and Drug Administration

(FDA) for the treatment of depression in children under 12. This does not mean that the FDA disapproves of such use. In fact, the FDA *has* approved imipramine (Tofranil) and nortriptyline (Pamelor) for investigational use in depressed children.

A considerable amount of research evidence indicates that these and other antidepressant medications can help alleviate depression and attention-deficit disorder in some children. Your doctor may therefore prescribe such drugs as part of a research study or if she feels antidepressants could be helpful to your child. Most doctors follow the position of the American Medical Association (AMA): "The prescription of a drug for an unlabeled indication is entirely proper if based on rational scientific theory, reliable medical opinion, or controlled clinical trials."

Tricyclic Antidepressants

The tricyclic antidepressants (TCAs) are named for a three-ring chain in their chemical structure. The following TCAs are most frequently prescribed to treat depression in children and adolescents: imipramine (Tofranil), amitriptyline (Elavil), desipramine (Norpramin), and nortriptyline (Pamelor). These medications work by correcting an imbalance in neurotransmitters, important chemical messengers within the brain.

Antidepressant medications are not "uppers," that is, they have no mood-altering effects on people who are not depressed, and they are neither habit-forming nor addictive. But when a person's brain chemicals are out of balance, antidepressants *can* help relieve the resulting symptoms—depressed mood, insomnia, fatigue, and loss of appetite—by restoring the balance. About three out of four children treated with adequate doses will respond positively to antidepressant medication.

Perhaps because of hormonal changes, adolescents don't always respond as well as children or adults do to TCAs. But some adolescents benefit from medications, so they may be suggested for your teenager.

MAKING THE DECISION Your child's psychiatrist should explain clearly why medication represents a good choice in terms that both you and your child can understand. Since medications are intended to relieve symptoms, I like to agree on the target symptoms with both parents and children. A child's sense of his symptoms may differ from the clinical report, but I encourage children to list in their own words a few things they would like to see change. For example, a depressed child may mention things like "feeling lonely all the time" or "getting stomachaches a lot."

When you talk to your child's psychiatrist about using antidepressant medications, inquire about the drug's possible benefits and how long it may take to achieve them. Ask what the short- and long-term negative side effects might be and find out how commonly they occur. If you or your child feels opposed to medication, or has serious doubts that may lead you to reduce or discontinue using medication prematurely, be sure to discuss these fully with the doctor rather than keeping them to yourself.

After a thorough discussion of medication pros and cons and a notion of your child's expected response, you'll have a better idea of what to expect and what to watch out for. I always try to use the lowest possible dose that produces the desired result.

I prefer to begin treatment with a low dose of medication for several reasons. First, some patients will respond fully to a low medication dose. Second, adverse reactions will usually be less severe on a lower dose. Third, a child gets a chance to get used to or even get over certain side effects before we raise the dose. Fourth, too high an initial dose can cause side effects and lead to terminating a drug that might have been tolerated well at a lower dose.

Then I can slowly but steadily raise the dose until all the symptoms abate, until side effects become too unpleasant, or until the maximum allowable dosage has been reached. If a particular drug achieves no significant benefit or if unacceptable side effects emerge, I reconsider the diagnosis and suggest a trial of a different medication.

Your child's doctor will probably suggest a specific medication based not only on your child's diagnosis, but also on a particular medication's side effects. Some antidepressants, for example, have greater sedating effects than others. These may be especially chosen for bedtime use if your child has difficulty sleeping.

But since some children appear to metabolize the medication faster, they may need to take smaller doses two or three times a day. Children with attention-deficit disorder and depression, for example, seem to do better on divided doses of antidepressants, some given during the day and the rest given at bedtime.

In addition, your child's doctor will probably ask about how your child or other family members have responded to related medications in the past. That's because if a close relative responded well to a certain medication, your child may be more likely to benefit from the same one.

Although you and your child may notice improvements in sleep and appetite within a few days, remember that TCAs usually take a few weeks to work optimally. The most common reason for medication failure is that too low a dose was tried for too short a time. Give a particular medication six to eight weeks at full dosage before concluding that it's not working.

At the suggestion of his pediatrician, Steven came to my office with his grandmother. The 12-year-old had been depressed for months. He described trouble falling asleep at night; a restless, fitful sleep that left him tired throughout the day; listlessness and lack of energy; and a minimal appetite. Steven hadn't lost any weight, but he had failed to gain weight despite a growth spurt in height.

Steven was living with his grandmother because the boy's father had abandoned the family when he was 2, and his mother had died in a car accident that may have been suicide two years ago. After talking to both Steven's pediatrician and his sixth-grade teacher, I concluded that the boy was indeed depressed, and suggested several ways we could approach treatment.

I explained the role of counseling and the possibility that medication might help as well. Both Steven and his grandmother felt uneasy about medication, so we decided to try psychotherapy alone for a while first, and we agreed to reevaluate in six weeks to see how much it helped.

Steven completed a Beck Depression Inventory, a questionnaire that asks about specific depressive symptoms. We planned to use it again in six weeks to note his progress.

Counseling helped somewhat, but six weeks later Steven still complained of feeling tired all the time, experiencing difficulty sleeping at night, and having little appetite. Steven's Beck score had dropped a little, but he still remained in the depressed range.

When we discussed the pros and cons of medication again, Steven decided he wanted to give it a try. To help the boy make his own appraisal of the medication, I encouraged him to create his own rating chart, including the symptoms that were most troubling to him. Steven listed things like "feeling tired all the time," "being bored a lot," and "not caring what happens." Then he rated each from 1 (negative) to 10 (positive) and we put the chart in his file.

We gradually increased Steven's dose over two weeks, and he tolerated the medication well without many side effects. The first thing Steven noticed was that he slept better. His grandmother remarked that his appetite had picked up within a week. After a month, Steven's mood improved and he began to participate more actively in his therapy. The boy showed continued improvement for about 10 weeks.

Steven remained on the antidepressant for five months, until the school year was over. Then we discontinued the medication and he has stayed symptom-free for three years. Steven continued to see his therapist weekly through the school year, and then just once a month until he was settled into seventh grade. Now he just sees her from time to time if he has a particular problem he wants to discuss.

SIDE EFFECTS   The main side effects of TCAs include drowsiness, blurred vision, dry mouth, weight gain, difficulty urinating, rapid heartbeat, and dizziness that may be related to lowered blood pressure. Since different TCAs have somewhat different side effects, I may suggest a new one if a child cannot tolerate the side effects of a particular drug. Some side effects are merely annoying, while others require prompt medical attention.

Side Effects That Should Be Reported to Your Child's Doctor

blurred vision or eye pain	seizures
confusion	problems urinating
fainting	skin rash and itching
hallucinations	shakiness
irregular heartbeat	sore throat and fever

Side Effects That May Not Require Medical Attention

These side effects often go away during treatment, but if they should persist, contact your child's doctor:

constipation	dizziness
increased appetite for sweets	nausea
drowsiness	tiredness or weakness
dry mouth	unpleasant taste
headache	weight gain or loss

Youngsters often experience fewer troublesome side effects than adults do. Many effects, like dry mouth or an unpleasant taste, disappear within a few days or can be easily remedied. To alleviate a dry mouth, for example, I recommend sugar-free candy, gum, or drinks.

Other effects, such as drowsiness, dizziness, and nausea, can also usually be easily resolved. To make drowsiness into a benefit, I suggest to most of my patients that they take their medications before bedtime.

Since the commonest time to get dizzy is when you stand up quickly, I advise children to take it a little slower if they feel dizzy or to linger for a moment at the edge of the bed before they hop out in the morning.

If medication gives your child a queasy stomach, have him try taking the medication with a little food, perhaps some crackers. Make sure your child brushes his teeth after eating though, because antidepressant medication can reduce saliva, and saliva rinses teeth and helps fight cavities.

Antidepressants rarely cause serious cardiovascular side effects. But since these drugs can affect the heart's rate or rhythm, any child who receives TCA treatment for depression should first have an electrocardiogram (EKG) to provide a baseline heart recording. Your doctor may repeat the EKG periodically while your child is on medication, especially if the dosage changes.

Your doctor may also want to check blood levels of the medication. That way everyone can be sure that your child is actually taking the medication as prescribed and that the dose is producing adequate blood levels.

Many medications prescribed for depression interact with other prescribed or over-the-counter medications, as well as with alcohol and recreational drugs. In treating adolescents, this can pose a serious risk: What you don't know can hurt! Let your child's psychiatrist know about any other drugs your child currently takes and be sure to consult your child's doctor before giving your depressed child any other medication.

Other Drugs

LITHIUM   If your depressed child fails to respond to a tricyclic antidepressant, her doctor may prescribe lithium to enhance the TCA's antidepressant effect. More commonly, however, lithium is used to treat bipolar disorder in children, adolescents, or adults. Lithium has proved effective both during acute manic episodes and to prevent their recurrence.

Lithium is generally given as a tablet or capsule by mouth two or three times a day. The proper dosage must be determined by measuring lithium levels in the blood, frequently at first while the proper dosage is being determined, and less frequently once a stable dose has been established.

Common side effects include increased thirst, increased fluid intake, and increased urination. Some children experience stomach upset or diarrhea and some gain weight on this medication.

Signs that the level of lithium may be too high or even toxic include vomiting, slurred speech, sedation, an unsteady gait, or changes in mental alertness and awareness.

Although lithium is a safe and effective medication when used properly, you should discuss its various risks and side effects with your child's doctor before starting this medication. Your child should certainly be informed about the nature and purpose of this medication in a way that he can readily understand.

Prior to starting lithium, your child's doctor will probably want to do some simple laboratory tests. These include a complete blood count, blood chemistries, and thyroid function tests. A urinalysis can identify possible medical causes of manic symptoms as well as verify that your child's kidneys can tolerate the drug. An electrocardiogram may also be ordered.

When an acute manic episode is accompanied by severe psychotic symptoms, such as auditory hallucinations and grandiose or paranoid delusions, an antipsychotic medication may be used along with lithium during the acute phase to relieve these symptoms more quickly.

If your child cannot tolerate lithium or the drug fails to produce the desired effect, his doctor may prescribe Carbamazepine. Originally an anticonvulsant, this drug has helped some children or adolescents with bipolar disorder.

OTHER ANTIDEPRESSANTS   Atypical depressions in adults, marked by hypersomnia and overeating, have been successfully treated with monoamine oxidase inhibitors (MAOIs). In addition to sharing some of the common side effects of TCAs, however, MAOIs interact negatively with many common foods, such as cheeses, yogurt, and sour cream. The taking of MAOIs therefore requires a strictly controlled diet. Newer antidepressants, such as fluoxetine (Prozac), are currently undergoing trials to demonstrate their safety and effectiveness for depressed children and adolescents.

10

SHOULD YOU HOSPITALIZE YOUR DEPRESSED CHILD?

___

Trisha maintained a straight-A average while starring on her high school's championship diving team. As a senior, Trisha was poised to compete in the state finals and perhaps even progress to a national contest. Instead of beginning the season with her team, however, Trisha took a whole bottle of Tylenol and didn't tell anyone for nearly 24 hours. The 16-year-old almost died.

After four days in intensive care, Trisha was transferred to our mental health unit. Ashamed of what she'd done and sorry to have put her parents through such agony, the teenager remained quite depressed. On the surface, this hard-driving, perfectionistic girl seemed to have unlimited confidence, but Trisha suffered from the nagging fear that she really wasn't good enough.

In the hospital, Trisha worked hard to beat her depression. She soon began to talk openly in groups and with her counselor about her feelings of self-doubt.

Trisha was very protective of her parents, insisting that they were "the best parents anyone could ever have." But once she realized that no one intended to blame them for her problems, the teen admitted that her parents had awfully high, perhaps unrealistic, expectations for her. For their part, Trisha's parents began to recognize in family discussions that they had expected their daughter to accomplish all the things they had failed to achieve themselves.

Trisha remained in the hospital for two weeks and participated in outpatient therapy for some months afterwards. As she grew steadily more healthy and independent, Trisha resumed diving. But now, for the first time, Trisha felt she was performing for herself rather than for everybody else.

A temporary hospitalization provided a safe haven for Trisha to begin looking at the desperate feelings that had led her to try to take her own life. As Trisha commented several months later, "I hated the idea of staying in the hospital, but I needed to be there. I was falling apart, but I was too busy to see it. In the hospital everything stopped long enough for me to get control again."

Most depressed children and adolescents can be treated outside the hospital. But under certain circumstances— attempted suicide, for example—hospitalization may offer an essential treatment alternative for your child.

Not so long ago, many psychiatrists believed that a seriously depressed child such as Trisha should be removed from the "harmful influence" of her family and kept in the hospital for as long as it took to restructure her psychologically—perhaps six months to a year. Then the child might be sent to a residential facility for another year or two. Today a suicidal adolescent such as Trisha will usually undergo a brief psychiatric hospitalization, followed by outpatient treatment that welcomes the family as an important force for change.

As the parent of a depressed child, you should learn exactly why hospitalization may be recommended for your child. Understanding the disadvantages as well as the advantages of hospitalization will enable you to make an informed decision about whether your child needs this placement.

We'll go through all the steps in the decision-making process, describing children who did and did not need to be hospitalized and suggesting some alternative options. The information in this chapter should enable you to participate actively in this very important decision.

WHY HOSPITALIZE YOUR DEPRESSED CHILD?

Hospitalization may be recommended or you may feel it's the right placement for your depressed child for any of the following reasons:

- His behavior endangers himself or others.
- He has failed to make progress in outpatient treatment.
- He simply can't function at home, in school, or with friends.
- His depression complicates the treatment of a serious physiological illness, or a physiological illness complicates the treatment of his depression.

Drawbacks to Hospitalization

Whether or not you eventually decide to put your depressed child in the hospital, you should know that even a necessary hospitalization can carry some significant drawbacks.

A NEGATIVE MESSAGE   For example, hospitalizing your child may send her the message that she's out of control or incapable of functioning in the outside world. Which she may well be, at least temporarily. But we want to convey confidence in the child's ability to regain control.

Adolescents may feel like hospitalization means punishment. Indeed, your depressed adolescent is probably already feeling guilty about many things that aren't her fault, perhaps even about being depressed. The teen who feels punished by a necessary hospitalization needs to be told that it is for her protection and represents punishment no more than an appendectomy would if she had appendicitis.

Some parents hear the recommendation to hospitalize their child as an indictment of their own parenting behavior, proving that they cannot take care of their own child. Of course, this is not the point. When it's necessary, hospitalization should be embraced by the entire family as the very best way to meet the child's needs at the time.

SOCIAL STIGMA   Although much less so today than even a few years ago, psychiatric hospitalization can be stigmatizing, or at least parents and children fear it will be. But, like any other negative event in life, you and your child should be able to work this through with the help of a sensitive therapist.

LOSS OF FREEDOM   Hospitalization certainly entails giving up some autonomy and control. This frightens adolescents more than it does younger children. Realizing this, the psychiatric hospital staff usually strives to preserve as much of your hospitalized child's ability to control his own circumstances as possible.

THE HOSPITAL MILIEU   Although peer pressure that is therapeutically channeled can be helpful in treating a depressed child, contact with other seriously troubled children can cause occasional problems. Be sure to discuss the general makeup of the psychiatric unit with your child's doctor, who will attempt to match your child with a unit and a group of other children who will be helpful rather than harmful to your child.

DISTANCE   If your child must be hospitalized far from home, your opportunity to be involved may be limited. Teenagers in particular often find it a hardship to have less contact with their friends.

EXPENSE   Finally, hospital treatment costs a lot of money and will probably be a significant drain on your family's resources. Even a brief hospitalization can consume limited funds which might have bought significantly more treatment in an alternative outpatient program.

Advantages of Hospitalization

In certain cases, however, hospitalization may offer the best possible solution for your family. The control a hospital provides could mean the difference between life and death if your child is suicidal, chemically dependent, or chronically truant. In addition, a hospital can offer medical supervision, concentrated therapy, a safe haven, a necessary rest, and structure to the child or adolescent who needs it.

MEDICAL SUPERVISION   A child who requires complex treatment for medical problems may be helped by a brief hospitalization, especially if his depression has prompted self-neglect or intentional self-injury.

For example, a pediatrician asked me to see Peter, a 12-year-old juvenile-onset diabetic who was hospitalized on the pediatric ward because his diabetes had gone out of control. Peter knew how to self-administer his insulin, but he vacillated between insistence on managing his illness on his own and total dependence, especially after periods of prolonged high blood sugar.

Ever since his diagnosis the year before, Peter had ignored his diet. At times, the boy almost seemed to go out of his way to eat the candy, pop, and junk foods that made his blood sugar soar. When his parents insisted that he check his blood sugar, Peter would go into the bathroom and say he had checked his urine without actually doing so.

Peter clearly rejected his illness and resented the limitations it placed on him. But he was also depressed. Like many other children with a serious chronic illness, Peter felt as though he had lost a part of himself. In his angrier moments, the boy shouted that his life was ruined before he had even had a chance to live it. Peter's depression certainly stemmed from his illness, but it soon began to aggravate the diabetes as well. The two conditions reinforced each other and took over Peter's life. In fact, they almost ended his life.

After five days on the pediatric unit, Peter's blood sugar came back under control. Then he spent two more weeks in the adolescent mental health unit, where his treatment plan combined medicine and psychiatry. Diabetic education taught Peter to manage his illness within a teenage lifestyle, and psychological treatments began helping Peter cope with his justifiable anger, sorrow, and loss.

Peter went home in charge of his own diet, insulin injections, and blood sugars. Instead of maintaining the futile struggle with his parents, Peter began reporting to a nurse who specialized in adolescent diabetes. This nurse, a sensitive but no-nonsense young woman who was diabetic herself, freed Peter's parents of their policing function and allowed them to resume a more enjoyable relationship with their son.

Some depressed children need antidepressant medication, which can be safer and easier to introduce in the controlled setting of a hospital (see Chapter 9). There doctors can monitor side effects, assess your child's compliance with the medication regimen, work through any resistance, and measure his response.

CONCENTRATED THERAPY   Almost no outpatient alternative can match the intensity of care available in a well-staffed hospital. At the hospital, your child will get 24-hour one-to-one care if she needs it. Most hospitalized children attend therapeutic sessions several times a day. In addition, group and family therapy occur frequently during the week. The intensity and sheer quantity of treatment make it hard for a hospitalized child to continue to avoid facing her problems and to resist making changes in herself.

In the hospital setting, all your child's problem behaviors or depressed feelings can be addressed immediately, while they are still fresh. This means feelings and memories no longer have to wait several days to be served up, reheated, in therapy. In an ideal setting, staff members may even be able to anticipate maladaptive behaviors and can suggest alternatives before they occur.

Therapists refer to the strategy of "bringing it into the room": re-enacting conflicts in the therapy session. A pattern of interaction that actually occurs in a therapy session can be modified much more easily than a pattern that is merely discussed. Although your hospitalized child may attempt for a time to act differently on the ward, her characteristic behaviors will soon appear in her daily interactions with peers, staff members, therapists, and doctors. Once your child's problem appears "live and in color" on the unit, we can address it and usually find a workable solution.

For example, 15-year-old Jason insisted that he was only depressed because his parents constantly nagged him and his teachers treated him like a baby. Jason claimed that if everyone would simply leave him alone he'd be fine.

For the first few days on the unit we did just that. We let Jason do his schoolwork on his own time and in his own way, and although he was "invited" to therapy groups and activities, no one insisted that he attend.

When reinforcement of a negative behavior such as non-compliance ceases, at first the behavior often worsens for a

time, as if the child desperately wants to get you to react
the way people always have before. Accordingly, Jason
began by doing little, and soon was doing even less. Some
of the staff wanted to jump in at this point and push him to
do his schoolwork and attend the groups. I suggested we
watch and wait, resisting the temptation to repeat the
same tactics that had failed to work for his parents and
teachers.

After a few days, Jason began to appear at group time,
saying he was "bored to death" in his room all day. When
we accepted his attendance without fanfare, Jason became
increasingly provocative in group. He undermined the
process, disrupted the conversation, and appeared to
be asking for discipline. But rather than expelling him
from group because of his behavior, we simply pointed out
what Jason was doing and suggested that he might be
behaving in ways at home and in school that provoked
adult intervention.

Jason responded well to the confrontation and inter-
pretation he received in the therapy group. And his behavior rapidly began to change. Over a period of several
weeks, Jason showed increased initiative, finally beginning
to take responsibility for his own life and his own work.
After Jason returned home, his parents needed a lot of
support not to jump in when he slipped, but rather simply
to confront him and let him take the consequences of his
own behavior.

A SAFE HAVEN   If a child's home or neighborhood poses a
threat to his safety, a hospital can provide protection. For
example, Dale, 15, had been exploited by a 28-year-old
male "friend" and neighbor. The older man befriended the
lonely and depressed boy, giving him attention and gifts.
But as Dale became more involved and dependent, the
man used him, eventually involving him in criminal wire-
tapping. After being hospitalized, Dale reported that he

had been unable to break off his relationship with the neighbor because he feared for his and his mother's safety.

RESPITE Perhaps most important of all, hospitalization can offer an enforced rest to a severely troubled or suicidal child. Even a tenaciously defiant child who seems to find endless ways to break rules and oppose your wishes may be physically and psychologically exhausted. Just dealing with the barrage of sensory and psychological input in a young person's daily world—blaring music, TV and videos advertising sex and violence, the provocations of peers, the never-ending demands of teachers, the sheer volume of information to be understood—can be daunting. For a seriously depressed child it can be overwhelming.

STRUCTURE The hospital environment strategically limits the amount of input, reducing the number of decisions that must be made. For some children, the set structure of the hospital routine—times for waking and going to sleep; regular meals; enforced school and homework periods; firm rules with predictable consequences; prohibitions against fighting, swearing, drugs, and weapons—frees up the energy they need for healthy growth. Relieved of most of the burdens of daily life, your depressed child may finally be induced to look at herself and her behavior and to talk about her struggles instead of acting them out.

Hospitalization as Interruption

It may be helpful to think of hospitalization as a temporary intermission in your child's life. For some children, this interruption is positive, while for others it can have a negative effect.

Hospitalization will certainly put a halt to just about everything that is going on in your child's life. Hospitalizing your child could stop destructive patterns of criticism, conflict, and scapegoating. But it might also interfere with healthy family patterns of communication, negotiation, and cooperation.

Likewise, hospitalization can stop drug use for some adolescents, while in other cases it could actually be an unwelcome interruption of successful self-motivated abstinence.

Just as hospitalization may prevent unhealthy dependency, it can also interfere with healthy independence and autonomy. Hospitalization interrupts the normal adolescent tasks of separating from family, establishing and deepening ties to peers, using peers for healthy support, developing intimate relationships outside the home, and developing relationships with respected adults other than parents.

Since hospitalization introduces such a profound change for the adolescent and his world, making the decision to hospitalize involves determining whether that radical change will improve matters. Naturally, you want to put a stop to drug use, criminal or antisocial behavior, truancy, and running away. But you don't want to interrupt growing self-confidence, the development of healthy new friendships, the adaptive renegotiation of family relationships, and progress toward deepening communication.

Unfortunately, determining what you are interrupting may not be simple. Growth sometimes occurs through adversity, frustration, mistakes, and failure. Sadness or loss can also produce growth. With a supportive and committed family and a network of friends and skilled professionals, an adolescent can sometimes recover from a major depression or drug abuse outside the hospital, and the process can strengthen and deepen all those ties. But continued failure and deterioration may break those very same ties.

In addition, hospitalization provides just one mechanism to plan an interruption of a downward spiral. You should certainly also consider day hospital, foster placement, community group homes, and other alternatives. In certain cases, placement in a group home or the home of friends or relatives may better enable your child to avoid the emotional regression than can result from hospitalization.

Bear in mind, however, that short-term, crisis-oriented hospitalization and long-term hospitalization differ. Self-destructive or dangerous behavior may indicate the need for a very brief psychiatric hospitalization.

THE DECISION-MAKING PROCESS

In order to see whether hospitalization provides the best solution, you'll need to clearly define your child's problem. To help you do this, seek out a support system that includes your child's therapist, your family, your friends, and concerned others. With help from this group, you and your child can set some specific goals. Decide what you can expect hospitalization or any other treatment alternative to achieve and how you will know when it's time for your child to come home.

Defining the Problem

Since clearly defining the problem helps point toward a solution—perhaps hospitalization—your child's therapist should work with you and your child to reach a consensus about what the real issues are.

For example, one of Holly's problems was that the 12-year-old felt personally responsible and guilty about her mother's cancer. Inappropriate guilt about another's illness can be defined by asking questions like: When did it start? How often do you feel guilty? How many times a day do you think about it? For how long? Does it keep you from doing anything you'd like to do? You can also do something about this problem: a therapist can help Holly correct the irrational aspects of assuming guilt for someone else's cancer, and can explore and work to understand all the painful feelings stirred up by a mother's illness. Finally, you can tell when such a problem is gone.

Your child's definition of her own problem, of course, may differ from yours. When I ask parents to name their teenager's problem, they may say, "She's depressed" or "She has low self-esteem" or "She takes no responsibility." But when I ask their adolescent what's the problem, she frequently replies, "They're always on my case." Naturally, a therapist's alliance with the child or adolescent must begin with the child's view of the problem. Then they work together to figure out what the *child* can do differently so that her parents are not "always on her case."

Calling on Your Support System

The first psychiatric contact for you and your child may come not after months of therapy, but at a moment of crisis—a suicide attempt, for example. But like any crisis, this one presents an opportunity as well as a danger. You now have a chance to build a cooperative relationship with your child's new therapist. Indeed, the process of considering hospitalization can offer everyone involved a model for communicating thoughts and feelings, clarifying problems, negotiating differences, and making decisions.

If your child is already engaged in treatment, his therapist will probably be centrally involved in the decision about hospitalization. Whatever decision you reach with your child's therapist, you and your child should feel that your thoughts and feelings are respected, your opinions valued, and that you are expected to be an integral part of the treatment team.

Your child's reactions to the therapist's recommendations should be thoroughly discussed and understood. Sometimes a child will ask directly for help, but more often he simply behaves in a way that causes the adults around him to do something. Still, being involved in the decision to the extent that he is able can help give him a sense of control and engage his future cooperation. If you and your child's therapist decide on hospitalization, you and your child should both feel that his problems are taken seriously, that his call for help has been heard, and that things will soon start to get better.

If you are separated or divorced, don't exclude your child's noncustodial parent from the decision-making process. If you do, he may react negatively to feeling left out and later become involved in an adversarial way. Even if you consider your spouse to be part of the problem, offer him a chance to be part of the solution. Sometimes siblings can also offer a unique perspective, different from yours or your child's.

Your rabbi, priest, or minister may be helpful in this process, especially if he knows your family well. Relatives and close friends who are important to you or your child can also participate in supporting you before and during your child's hospitalization. Indeed, anyone who has had or will have a relationship with your child and is committed to promoting his development may lend a hand. This list can include teachers, counselors, lawyers, probation officers.

Though they are frequently ignored by mental health professionals, friends can be a crucial additional resource. Adolescents, especially, rely on their friends for advice and support.

Brandon's friends, for example, brought the 16-year-old boy in for treatment. Morbidly depressed and preoccupied with thoughts of suicide, Brandon lacked sufficient energy to carry out his plan. Brandon's mother lived in another state and rarely contacted him. His father was self-absorbed, ad-

dicted to his work, and rarely home. The boy usually ate a
TV dinner by himself and read until he fell asleep at night.

Brandon's friends noticed something had changed when
the teen lost his sense of humor, started drinking a lot on
weekends, and began to pick fights for no reason. Though
his friends mentioned their concern to his father, he did
nothing.

So Brandon's friends finally brought him in for treatment themselves. One of them knew me from a talk I had
given at her high school and tracked me down one day at
the hospital to ask if she could bring a friend right over to
see me. I met the teenagers at the hospital and spoke to
Brandon for a long while. Indeed, the boy was depressed to
the point of imminent suicide. After I contacted his father,
we admitted Brandon to the hospital that very night.

Brandon's friends stayed involved throughout the two
weeks he was in the hospital. They visited him frequently,
participated in support groups that were open to family
and friends, brought him notes from his school classes, and
eased his transition back to regular school. Like family in
the best sense of the word, Brandon's friends certainly
played a key role in his recovery.

Involving relatives and friends in the decision about
hospitalization can make them feel enthusiastic about taking part in a collaborative treatment process. Beginning
with the decision to hospitalize your child, their support
will continue throughout the hospitalization and should
extend well beyond it.

Setting Goals

Once you have identified specific problems and called on
your support system, set some attainable goals. These can
help you determine which kind of treatment, including
hospital treatment, will be most appropriate for your
child.

Goals vary. Holly's father's goal was that his daughter could come to terms with her mother's terminal illness soon enough that she could stop acting out her fear and rage and finally say goodbye to her dying mother. One adolescent's main goal was to build a different kind of relationship with his stepfather so that his stepfather would no longer view him as defiant and so that he could feel more accepted by the man.

Most goals fall into one of the following five categories: crisis intervention, assessment, support and engagement, change, and termination. Determine your own goals with your child's therapist and your support network to see how you can best achieve them.

CRISIS INTERVENTION   Treatment in a crisis attempts to halt self-destructive behavior and prevent injury to the child and others. Criminal activity, drug and alcohol abuse, and running away must be terminated immediately for the sake of the adolescent, her family, and the community. Though hospitalization can serve this purpose, in certain cases I have succeeded by combining a 24-hour-a-day watch by the family with intensive crisis therapy.

Such profound family involvement frequently leads to exciting changes. After spending most of 48 hours one-to-one with his suicidal son, one father reported, "I talked more to John this weekend than I had in five years. I didn't know him until now. I've gotten to know my son and it has changed us both. We'll never be the same again."

ASSESSMENT   When I sit down with a family to discuss their child's hospitalization, we usually identify problems that require further assessment. I sometimes find the hospital the best place to observe firsthand a child's emotional state, his behavior, his ability to communicate his thoughts in a variety of situations, and his ability to relate to others.

Often a child is referred by his school because he is causing trouble, failing, or not attending classes. School problems may be related to intellectual limitations, a learning disability, depression, anxiety, distraction, drug use, fatigue, fear, or many other factors. Hospitalization in a program that has a therapeutic school and testing for learning disabilities can sometimes make it easier to assess, diagnose, and treat these problems. But the hospital-school environment differs radically from that of regular school. A hospital school is much more structured, with most distractions screened out.

Deciding whether to use hospitalization for such an assessment therefore depends on whether a "laboratory" setting or a "naturalistic" setting will reveal more about your child. In the hospital we can control many, although certainly not all, variables in the environment for a more focused look at certain problems. On the other hand, evaluating a child's behavior and functioning in his natural environment may offer a more realistic view.

A full assessment of your child would include his physical health and development, personal strengths, coping mechanisms, conscience, self-control, and self-esteem. Indeed, assessment should address itself to the entire constellation of your child's thoughts, feelings, behaviors, and relationships, with the ultimate goal of helping him. Discuss with your child's therapist whether this assessment can be better done within the hospital or outside.

Support and Engagement   Hospitalization provides the maximum amount of external support and guidance for a severely disturbed child or adolescent. But such support should be provided only in such amount and for as long as the child needs it.

Think about a continuum of structure—a range of services that can be used to provide structure for a child in distress. Structure, of course, is the organizing framework by which people process information, deal with stress, and relate to others. In the course of normal development, children and adolescents build up this structure inside themselves. But some children lack internal structure. Either a child had it and it collapsed under stress, or perhaps she never developed it. A seriously depressed child may benefit from a brief hospitalization because the inpatient hospital provides a complete replacement structure for the one she lacks: walls to limit where she can go, rules to govern appropriate behavior, procedures for doing what she's supposed to, and people to help her deal with any strong feeling that threatens to become overwhelming.

The hospital stands at one end of the continuum, with living at home and going to a regular school at the other end. Obviously families vary in the amount of structure they provide, from very little to quite a bit. Furthermore, some children reject any amount of structure, disregarding their curfews and family rules, cutting classes, and skipping school. On the continuum of structure between home and the psychiatric hospital lie day or evening hospital and intensive outpatient programs. These moderate-structure alternatives allow a child or adolescent to live at home and perhaps even to attend regular school, but they provide additional support and services for several hours a day through the week. Such alternatives can serve children or teenagers who are able to attend regular school, participate in an outpatient program, and abide by some fundamental rules at home.

The supportive function of hospitalization includes relief. If a child or adolescent can sleep no more than three hours a night, or if a family is exhausted from the task of enforcing discipline in their home, they need prompt relief in order to recover and proceed toward their goals.

For example, Tom, a 15-year-old delinquent, came from a family that consistently set limits and followed through with consequences. But their son's behavior was so aggressive, his parents often had to physically restrain him from leaving the house when he was grounded. Controlling him usually took two parents and it sometimes required staying up all night. When they finally brought Tom to the hospital, his parents were completely exhausted. Our first goal of hospitalization was to give some relief to Tom's family.

We had considered alternatives such as enlisting relatives or friends to help out with supervision, or even placing Tom temporarily with another family. But the boy was beginning to manifest psychotic symptoms and his behavior had turned increasingly violent. We decided on hospitalization to provide a locked, safe environment and to undertake a trial of antipsychotic medication.

Yet even in this case, Tom's family maintained a sense of competence because they participated fully in the decision about their son's placement. During his hospitalization, Tom's family actively helped to plan his discharge and return home.

CHANGE   Parents considering hospitalization for their depressed children usually seek some sort of major alteration. You may hope to correct a "chemical imbalance" with medication. You may want to see a change in your child's behavior or an improvement in her functioning at school. Your child's therapist may refer her for hospitalization because outpatient therapy has thus far been unsuccessful.

If you've identified family problems, your goal may be to develop a workable family hierarchy, in which parents share leadership and children get age-appropriate privileges and responsibilities. Your child or adolescent may need to learn effective problem-solving skills or to improve social skills and social relationships. Hospitalization or any other kind of treatment should promote your child's identity, self-esteem, autonomy, self-control, and empathy for others.

As you weigh the important decision of whether to hospitalize your child, make a list of the changes you want to accomplish. Consider whether a brief hospitalization will be more likely to help or hinder these changes.

For example, will hospitalization increase or decrease your child's self-control and self-esteem? If your child exercises appropriate self-control and feels good about that, taking away her autonomy may damage her self-esteem. But if she is overwhelmed by distractions and impulses, or if she has lost control of her behavior and doesn't know how to get it back, the temporary support and external control of a hospital may actually preserve her dignity.

If your adolescent communicates effectively with at least a few people and if she relates well to some dependable others, she may be able to form a working therapeutic alliance outside the hospital. Hospitalization could disrupt the network she has built. But if her behavior is so disturbed or her communication is so poor that all her relationships have deteriorated, then hospitalization might prevent irreparable harm and teach her some adaptive social skills in a protected setting.

Change actually begins during the process of making the decision about hospitalization. In the process of defining the problems, setting goals for change, and selecting treatment, you and your child can deepen your understanding of each other and make a firm commitment to work together.

TERMINATION   The ultimate goal of treatment, of course, is to get your child back to healthy, independent functioning within his family, school, and community. Depending on the real resources available to you at the time of crisis, you may or may not choose hospitalization as the best means to this end.

For example, Eddie, a suicidal adolescent, was referred by his school for possible hospitalization. When we discussed the issues producing the crisis and the pros and cons of hospitalization, Eddie's parents finally understood the seriousness of their son's problems and his desperation. Consulting with Eddie, they convened a support network of family, neighbors, and several of his friends that same night. They reconnected with a therapist they had seen two years before, who agreed to work with them on an intensive basis during this crisis, beginning the very next day. Eddie's father took a one-week leave from his job to supervise and work intensively with his son. Eddie was successfully treated outside the hospital.

In trying to identify your own resources, ask yourself the following questions:

- Do you really have the time and the knowledge you'll need to support your child in crisis and ensure that he follows through with treatment recommendations?
- Does his school have the facilities and the expertise to provide supportive services outside the hospital?
- Does a competent therapist have the time and the interest to treat your child on an outpatient basis?

On the other hand, you must also determine whether the hospital you are considering really offers an appropriate therapeutic program for your child's particular problems. The needs of a depressed, suicidal 13-year-old girl differ radically from those of a delinquent, paranoid 17-year-old boy. You should choose a hospital based on its treatment approach, staff, program strengths, and current patient population.

Like Eddie, 13-year-old Jennifer also revealed suicidal plans in school. But Jennifer had very few resources. Her divorced, alcoholic mother hesitated to come to school even after she was told of her daughter's suicidal behavior. Other family members refused to communicate at all, and several previous therapists resisted taking on this volatile family again. Jennifer was hospitalized for her own protection, but within a couple of weeks an elaborate support network of concerned family, neighbors, teachers, and two willing therapists arose. Only in the protected atmosphere of the hospital could we form a therapeutic contract with Jennifer's family.

Once you have considered the pros and cons of hospitalization for your child, you need to arrive at a conclusion.

Sometimes the very decision to hospitalize your child becomes a therapeutic event in itself. All the steps you have gone through in your decision-making process—defining problems, setting goals, and selecting appropriate treatment—represent important beginnings in the healing process.

11

CHOOSING THE BEST HOSPITAL

If your child requires hospitalization, you need to know how to find the very best hospital for him. It's also vital that you learn exactly what will happen to your child in the hospital setting so you can support his treatment and eventual homecoming. By following the suggestions outlined in this chapter, you'll be better able to participate positively in your child's hospital treatment and his eventual return home.

CHECKING YOUR INSURANCE

If you decide on hospitalization and your child's admission is not an emergency, be sure to find out exactly what your policy covers. The average cost of treating a child or adolescent in a private psychiatric hospital—including room and board plus therapy and medications—exceeded $20,000 in 1990, with an average stay of 34 days for adolescents and 39 days for children. Many insurance policies put a yearly or even a lifetime cap of $10,000 on psychiatric benefits.

Call your insurance agent and state your policy number, the name of the person who is insured, and where the subscriber works. Or phone the personnel office where you or your spouse works and ask to speak with someone about precisely what your policy covers.

Since dependent coverage may differ from employee coverage, find out whether and for how long your child is covered under your policy. Usually, a child can receive coverage from his parent's health insurance until the end of the calendar year in which he reaches 19, unless he is enrolled in college. If your depressed child is almost 19, you may be able to institute procedures to extend his coverage.

In the rapidly changing field of health insurance, many employers and insurance companies have reduced benefits to contain costs. Companies may add, subtract, or change insurance carriers and health plans frequently, so you'll need to get up-to-date information from your current insurer.

Ask the following questions:

- What is the annual mental health coverage? for inpatient treatment? for outpatient treatment?
- What percentage of charges will be paid?
- What is the deductible per year? per policy period?
- What is the lifetime maximum?
- Are there any exclusions? (conduct disorders or eating disorders may be excluded, for example)
- Are pre-existing conditions excluded?
- How many of the following services are covered:
  —psychological testing
  —individual therapy
  —group therapy
  —family therapy
  —multidisciplinary staffings
- How many of the following professionals are covered:
  —physicians

> —psychologists
> —social workers
> —others

- Are alternatives to inpatient hospitalization covered, such as day or evening partial hospitalization, or intensive outpatient programs?
- What coverage exists for alcohol and drug abuse?

Many insurance plans require a preadmission certification procedure before they will pay for psychiatric hospitalization. This usually involves a conference between a representative of your insurance company and your child's primary therapist to ascertain whether your child's illness warrants hospitalization.

If you belong to a health maintenance organization (HMO), a preferred provider organization (PPO), or a comprehensive health plan (CHP), your benefits may pay for only a very short hospital stay in a particular hospital. Be sure to determine exactly what your coverage will be.

SELECTING A HOSPITAL

Depending on your insurance and what you can afford to pay, you may have a wide or narrow array of hospitals to choose from. Possibilities include the psychiatric ward of a general hospital or public mental hospital, or a private psychiatric hospital.

As an alternative to public or private centers, some counties run their own hospitals, and so do many universities. Regardless of whether they are public or private and how much they cost, hospitals vary widely in the quality of care they offer.

When considering a hospital stay for your depressed child, look for a high-quality institution with a program specifically designed for emotionally disturbed children or adolescents. Ideally, the hospital should be close to your home and a place where you and your child can feel comfortable.

Do Some Research

Two accreditation agencies, the Joint Commission on Accreditation of Healthcare Organizations and the National Association of Private Psychiatric Hospitals, can let you know whether the hospitals you are considering have met a set of minimum standards. The American Academy of Child and Adolescent Psychiatry publishes guidelines for choosing a psychiatric hospital. The National Alliance for the Mentally Ill and the National Mental Health Association, two national groups with local affiliates, can also offer you the benefit of professional and personal recommendations on specific hospitals. (See the Resources section for the addresses of these five organizations.)

Next, find out whether the hospitals you are considering house and treat children and adolescents separately from adults. Depressed children and adolescents should be on their own floor or unit, treated by a specially trained staff.

Make a list of any specific questions you have about your child's placement and/or treatment. Talk to the therapist who will be in charge of coordinating your child's treatment to discuss exactly what the treatment goals and methods will be.

Let your child's therapist know you want to be as actively involved as you can and find out exactly how you can participate in your child's treatment. Find out who will be working with you as a family and how often you will have sessions. These should be at least once, and preferably twice, a week. Ask about parent support and education groups and when they meet.

You will want regular feedback on your child's progress and you should determine when this will take place. Ask, too, whether the hospital has a handbook to answer any questions you forget to ask. Things as simple as "What clothes should my daughter bring?" and "Can her friends call her on the telephone?" are useful for you to know.

Take a Tour

Next, visit the wards, the grounds, the cafeteria, and the school. If possible, bring your child along to see whether he would feel comfortable in this particular setting, but don't expect too much help from him. If your child is extremely depressed and apathetic he'll probably just say, "I don't care," and if he's irritable or defiant, he'll object to everything, accuse you of trying to get rid of him, or tell you, "This will just make me worse."

Sometimes, people try too hard to persuade a child to be enthusiastic about hospitalization. If he needs it, he needs it. You know it, his doctor knows it, and he probably knows it, too. But you must let him save face. Allow your child to use your insistence as a rationale for going into the hospital so that he doesn't have to openly confess his neediness and ask for help. He's vulnerable right now and he has a lot of mixed feelings. Openly asking for help probably feels childish to him.

Seth, 16, put it this way at the time of his discharge: "I needed to come in here; I know that now. At the time, I was really mad, at you sort of, but especially at my parents for putting me in here. I know I threw a fit in your office, but you notice I didn't really fight it. I didn't run away or anything and I easily could have. I could have even gotten out of the unit any time I wanted to. You think it's escape-proof but it's not—I could have broken out but I didn't."

Realizing that Seth needed to be recognized for cooperating, I replied, "I'm sure you could have figured out a way to get out, but it took a lot of guts to stay. You certainly deserve credit for that." Much less defensive now, and able to acknowledge what had threatened him before, Seth said, "You were right about one thing: I would have killed myself. And that would have been stupid. I'm glad I came here."

That, by the way, is about the most an adolescent will ever admit about the value of hospitalization. I don't hold my breath waiting for a patient to say, "Thank you, Doctor, for recognizing that I was depressed and out of control. I'm glad you took control for me temporarily and helped me feel better about myself."

On the wards, you should note plenty of evidence of personal belongings in the children's rooms. What do the children do all day? On a tour, you should see the children up and involved in treatment, school, and activities, and not simply sitting in their rooms.

Does the number of staff appear to be sufficient to deal with the number of children? How does the staff seem to interact with the children?

Do some of the children appear to be overmedicated? Is the temperature comfortable? Are there plenty of games and recreational activities available on the wards and grounds? Will the noise level be tolerable for your child?

Is there a seclusion room with a window? Can this whole room be seen from the outside for the child's safety? Note whether the bathrooms are clean and adequately stocked. Do the shower bars collapse under pressure (a suicide preventive)? Are all glass doors and windows shatterproof?

Watch the school in session. What is the child-teacher ratio? Will the teachers work closely with your child's own teachers so that she does not fall too far behind in her schoolwork?

At best, a psychiatric hospital can provide a therapeutic milieu where your child will receive intensive treatment for her depression. But remember that hospitalization is not a treatment in itself; it's merely a place where such treatment occurs. Take the time to find a setting that maintains staff who are qualified to treat your child and with whom you feel comfortable. If you can't communicate well with the hospital treatment team, it's the wrong place for your child to be treated. Likewise, if the hospital is too far away for you to take part meaningfully in your child's treatment, look for a high-quality setting closer to home.

WHAT HAPPENS IN THE HOSPITAL?

Ask about the schedule at the hospital that you are considering for your child. At the adolescent unit where I consult, wake-up occurs between 6:30 and 7:30 A.M. Children take showers, get dressed, make their beds, and pick up their rooms. Once they are ready for the day, they have about 10 minutes to make a telephone call if they want.

Breakfast lasts from 8 to 8:30. Some children eat in the community room on the unit, while others who have earned off-unit privileges may choose to go down to the hospital cafeteria and dining room.

Community meeting takes place from 8:30 to 9. At this meeting, patients and staff talk about the daily schedule. There they take care of community business; set goals for the day; assign duties like dayroom cleanup; and discuss and solve community problems. On a typical day, for example, the group might discuss some patients not showing respect for the rights of others. Once the community meeting is adjourned, the children gather their books and school materials in order to get to their classroom by 9.

Class time usually occupies three or four hours of a child's day. There he'll work on coursework from regular school as well as any supplementary programming that has been scheduled. A typical school session might run from 9 to noon with a 15-minute break about halfway through.

The children eat lunch from 12 to 12:30 and then attend a problem-solving group for the next half hour. This educa-

tional and role-playing group affords children the opportunity to define a problem, brainstorm about possible
solutions, make a decision, and evaluate the results.

The psychotherapy group meets for the following hour
or hour and a half. In group psychotherapy, one or two
staff members meet with a group of 6 to 10 children to talk
about a wide variety of issues and problem areas. They use
the group process to develop insight, encouraging positive
peer pressure to motivate change.

Children get an hour of quiet time after psychotherapy
group to think, read, or just relax. Then they spend the rest
of the afternoon in specialty groups. Some of these groups
are educational—communication skills group, for example—while others, like art therapy, are experiential. Late
in the afternoon, children get a structured exercise session
along with instruction in how to take better care of their
bodies and their health.

After a 5 o'clock dinner, children have a half hour or 45
minutes to make phone calls, catch up on homework, or
relax. For an hour before visiting time, children participate in specialty groups again, including drug and alcohol
education/prevention, self-awareness and self-esteem groups,
assertiveness education, and a family living group that
examines the positive and negative ways that families
interact.

The hours between 7 and 9 P.M. are prime time for
family involvement. Family therapy sessions often take
place then, as well as scheduled parent education and
training groups, and multiple-family group therapy.

All visitors usually leave by 9 P.M., when the entire
community of patients and staff gets together again for a
wrap-up group to review the day, deal with problems so
that the children can settle down for bed, and talk a little
about the next day. After wrap-up, children eat a snack,
tidy up the common areas of the unit, and then get ready
for bed. Adolescents typically are given an hour from 10
to 11 in which they can be in their rooms reading, studying,

or talking quietly with their roommate. Their lights go out at 11.

In addition to the activities described above, your child's treatment will probably also involve individual therapy with a psychiatrist or psychologist three to seven times a week to work on the problems that sent him to the hospital.

Compared to the time your child will spend at home, his stay in the hospital is fleeting. You all need to learn new ways of functioning for after he comes home. That's why I encourage considerable family involvement in the treatment process. Find out, for example, whether you can sit in on any of the therapeutic activities that occur throughout the day. I sometimes ask parents to participate in the psychoeducational assessment of their child so that they can understand as clearly as possible their child's unique ways of gathering, processing, and using information. Parents can also help develop behavioral plans and contracts and work with their children on the unit. Therapeutic home passes will help you and your child practice the new skills you are both learning as he gets ready to be discharged.

The Hospital School

Most psychiatric hospitals assess each child's educational needs in order to tailor-make an accredited educational program. Smaller hospitals may have an individual teacher come in to tutor your child, while larger hospitals usually house their own special schools. Class sizes tend to be small—perhaps two to eight students with each special-education teacher. An extension of the therapeutic environment, these hospital classes should help your child with problems such as focusing attention, setting realistic goals, and completing tasks. Usually the special-education teacher will stay in close contact with your child's regular teachers so that your child can keep up with her classwork. She should receive credit for the schoolwork she does in the hospital. After you learn the details of your child's educational program, see whether you can get together with the special-education teacher for a parent-teacher conference.

I like to schedule one staff meeting between the hospital staff and the child's regular schoolteachers and counselors at the beginning of hospitalization, to help us understand the school-related issues and to set common goals. We hold another staff meeting at the time of discharge to inform school personnel about the child's progress and to develop a coordinated treatment plan.

The Treatment Team

Your hospitalized child will most likely be treated by a team of mental health professionals with specialized skills. Your child's treatment team may include some or all of these people: psychiatrists, psychologists, clinical social workers, clinical nurse specialists, drug counselors, teachers, occupational therapists, dieticians, and general or specialty physicians.

WHAT YOU CAN DO

Some parents simply hospitalize their child and breathe a sigh of relief, as if she's someone else's problem now. In an extreme example of this attitude, a mother and father brought their 14-year-old daughter into the emergency room. Desperate and insistent that she be hospitalized because of depression and uncontrollable behavior, her parents left on a 10-day vacation cruise the next day!

You shouldn't think of the hospital as a place to get rid of your problem, because that will never happen without your participation. Instead, think of the hospital as a place to work on your problem. and be prepared to work hard.

You can help your child most by making a commitment to her treatment and getting as actively involved as you can. This will take time and energy as well as flexibility.

In the hospital your child will be going through a lot of changes, perhaps at lightning speed. She will be asked to examine herself repeatedly every single day. You need to be available to work with her and adapt as she changes. Be willing to change yourself, too.

Get ready to listen. In the hospital, your child will be encouraged to identify and express her thoughts and feelings, rather than keeping them all bottled up inside. She may be angry at you and she may tell you so for the first time, but try to take her anger in stride. Your child's candor doesn't mean that you've been a bad parent, that you have caused her to be depressed, or that your relationship with her is ruined. She may just need to get some strong feelings off her chest. You should know that children get angry with their parents just as parents sometimes get angry with each other. There may or may not even be any real reason for her anger. But you'll both survive it. And once you're able to be completely honest with each other, you'll find you can really improve your relationship.

Be patient. Hospital treatment is intensive, but patterns that have developed over years won't simply change overnight. Give the process a chance to work.

Do your homework. If your child's doctor or your family's therapist asks you to go home and make a list of responsibilities that you think are appropriate for a 12-year-old, then do it. Don't waste time and money by avoiding your responsibilities in the treatment process.

Try to cooperate with your child's other parent, too. Whether you're divorced or not, in agreement or disagreement, set your conflicts aside and work together to help your child through this temporary crisis.

WHEN IT'S TIME TO GO HOME

Your child can come home from the hospital when he is no longer dangerous to himself or anyone else and can safely be treated at a less intensive level of care. Before he goes home, a thorough plan will be developed for his outpatient care.

Of course, from very early in hospitalization you, your doctor, and the staff should be thinking about the "discharge plan." This is the blueprint for treatment after your child leaves the hospital and should include:

- Where your child will be living.
- Where he will be going to school.
- His course schedule, with classes planned in part on the basis of information obtained from his assessment in the hospital.
- A plan for using support services available through the school such as counseling and aftercare groups.
- A therapy plan including who he will see, how often, and for how long. Continued family therapy will usually be a part of this plan, too.

If your child is taking medications, ask for a plan for administering them at home, a review of potential side effects and problems, and an appointment for a follow-up visit with his doctor.

12

WHAT DOES THE FUTURE HOLD?

——

The future will most likely see society paying increased attention to the prevalence and importance of childhood depression. A variety of different research approaches are currently exploring many aspects of this serious illness.

Psychotherapy research, for example, currently struggles to answer the following questions:

Who benefits most from psychotherapy?
Which kind of therapy treats what kind of patient most effectively?
Do brief treatment methods work as well as longer-term therapy?
What makes a good match between therapist and patient?

Epidemiological investigation seeks to clarify how depression affects a variety of other problems: school difficulties, conduct disorders, eating disorders, and drug abuse. Genetic research aims to identify the specific mechanisms involved in inheriting the vulnerability to depression. One day, scientists may even be able to pinpoint the specific gene or genes responsible for some forms of this illness.

Ongoing inquiry into brain chemistry tries to provide increasingly more specific descriptions of the brain chemicals and neuroreceptors responsible for clinical depression. With a more specific understanding of brain dysfunction, researchers will be able to design more focused biological interventions.

Developments in the field of psychopharmacology will probably produce more effective antidepressant medications with fewer side effects.

You probably wonder whether your child will experience any long-term effects following her treatment for depression. Of course, no one can guarantee that any child's future life will be trouble-free. However, you and your child have learned to pay attention to key signs of depression and to look at her behavior and feelings in a new way. You both have every reason to feel hopeful about her future.

Here are four brief follow-up reports on depressed children whom you met in the pages of this book. Felice and John originally appeared in Chapter 2, Mark in Chapter 6, and Jocelyn in Chapter 9.

Felice

This 8-year-old girl had been devastated by her family's sudden transfer and separation from her best friend. In therapy, Felice finally admitted her grief over the move. Sessions with the therapist allowed Felice's parents, too, to explore their own reactions to this abrupt change in their lives. Felice's father, for example, spoke about how stunned he had been about losing his job and the extent to which this had wounded his self-esteem. To avoid feeling so vulnerable, he had shut himself off emotionally from his family. His wife talked about how scared she had been for him, for herself, and for their children. Like Felice, she mourned the loss of several close friends.

Once family members revealed these feelings to a therapist, they finally found themselves able to talk with each other. Then they could began to act. Felice's mother reached out to some women in her church and developed a few new friendships. Felice started to try to make friends by inviting some girls over. As she participated more actively in school, Felice resumed being the good student she had been before her depression. After three months of counseling, Felice's family felt more at home in their new community, and she had recovered completely from her depression.

John

After John, 16, experienced an acute episode of mania, he responded well to lithium treatment and psychotherapy. Several attempts to taper John off his medication brought on relapses of thought distortion, grandiosity, sleeplessness, and agitation. Since John tolerated the lithium without significant side effects, he continued taking the drug. At a three-year follow-up, John remained symptom-free and was functioning well at college.

Mark

This 16-year-old boy had been addicted to cocaine as a form of self-medication for depression. Though Mark's physical addiction was broken by a brief stay in a psychiatric hospital, the teenager remained deeply depressed. Mark used a 12-step recovery program combined with individual counseling and antidepressant medication to help him stay off cocaine and function on an even keel.

Mark's Narcotics Anonymous sponsor, a 21-year-old man with three years of sobriety, provided a good role model. Mark also participated in an adolescent support group that met near his home.

When Mark returned to his old high school in the fall following his hospitalization, he passed all his courses with C's and B's. Mark felt proud of this striking improvement in his grades. His part-time job at a camera store provided another source of self-esteem. Because Mark knew a lot about photography, he enjoyed advising customers about their choice of products such as film and lens filters. At a 24-month follow-up, Mark was still drug- and alcohol-free and his mood remained normal.

Jocelyn

This 15-year-old girl attended psychotherapy sessions for over a year. The year Jocelyn was in therapy for a suicidal depression, she earned the best grades she had ever received in school. As Jocelyn recovered from her depression, she expressed her newfound self-awareness by writing and painting, and she went on to achieve academic success in college. Two years after I last met with Jocelyn, I saw an exhibition of her paintings at a well-known art gallery.

I could tell countless other success stories of children who received timely and appropriate treatment for depression. The tragedies are stories of children whose depression went unrecognized or untreated.

In this book, I've detailed how depression, a serious illness, can interfere with your child's development. I've also maintained that, when recognized early, this illness can be very effectively treated. By paying attention and addressing your child's depression quickly, you have the power to save his very life and set him on a positive path for the future.

REFERENCES

___

Introduction

Gans, J. E. "America's Adolescents: How Healthy Are They?" *Profiles of Adolescent Health Series*, Volume 1. Chicago: American Medical Association, 1990.

Chapter 1: Childhood Depression: A Closer Look

Goertzel, Victor, and Mildred George Goertzel. *Cradles of Eminence*. Boston: Little, Brown, 1962.

Harrington, R. et al. "Adult Outcomes of Childhood and Adolescent Depression." *Archives of General Psychiatry* 47 (1990): 465.

McGlashan, T. H. "Comparison of Adolescent- and Adult-Onset Unipolar Depression." *American Journal of Psychiatry* 146 (1989): 1208.

Chapter 2: Is Your Child Depressed?

Golombek, Harvey. "Feeling States During Adolescence." *Psychiatric Clinics of North America* 13:3 (1990): 443–54.

Ivens, Carolyn, and Lynn Rehm. "Assessment of Childhood Depression: Correspondence Between Reports by Child, Mother, and Father." *Journal of the American Academy of Child and Adolescent Psychiatry* 27:6 (1988): 738–41.

McGlashan, T. H. "Adolescent Versus Adult Onset of Mania." *American Journal of Psychiatry* 145:2 (1988): 221.

McKnew, Donald, L. Cytryn, M. Lamour, and A. Apter. "Fantasy in Childhood Depression and Other Forms of Childhood Psychopathology." *Adolescent Psychiatry* 10 (1982): 292–98.

Offer, D., E. Ostrov, K. Howard, and R. Atkinson. "Normality and Adolescence." *Psychiatric Clinics of North America* 13:3 (1990): 377–88.

Puig-Antich, Joaquim, E. Lukens, M. Davies, D. Goetz, J. Brennan-Quattrock, and G. Todak. "Psychosocial Functioning in Prepubertal Major Depressive Disorders: I. Interpersonal Relationships During the Depressive Episode." *Archives of General Psychiatry* 42 (May 1985): 500–507.

———. "Psychosocial Functioning in Prepubertal Major Depressive Disorders: II. Interpersonal Relationships After Sustained Recovery from Affective Episode." *Archives of General Psychiatry* 42 (May 1985): 511–17.

Ryan, Neal, J. Puig-Antich, P. Ambrosini, H. Rabinovich, D. Robinson, B. Nelson, S. Iyengar, and J. Twomey. "The Clinical Picture of Major Depression in Children and Adolescents." *Archives of General Psychiatry* 44 (1987): 854–61.

Shaffer, David. "Suicide in Childhood and Early Adolescence." *Journal of Child Psychology and Psychiatry* 15 (1974): 275–91.

Spitz, R. A. "Anaclitic Depression: An Enquiry into the Genesis of Psychiatric Conditions in Early Childhood." *Psychoanalytic Study of the Child* 2 (1946): 313.

Varanka, T. et al. "Lithium Treatment of Manic Episodes with Psychotic Features in Prepubertal Children." *American Journal of Psychiatry* 145:12 (1988): 1557.

Winnicott, D. W. *The Maturational Processes and the Facilitating Environment*. New York: International Universities Press, 1965.

Chapter 3: Why Is Your Child Depressed?

Abramson, L. Y. et al. "Learned Helplessness in Humans: Critique and Reformulation." *Journal of Abnormal Psychology* 87 (1978): 47.

Beardslee, W. R., and D. Podorefsky. "Resilient Adolescents Whose Parents Have Serious Affective and Other Psychiatric Disorders: The Importance of Self-Understanding and Relationships." *American Journal of Psychiatry* 145 (1988): 63.

Beck, A. T. et al. *Cognitive Therapy for Depression*. New York: Guilford Press, 1979.

Bowlby, John. "Grief and Mourning in Infancy and Early Childhood." *Psychoanalytic Study of the Child* 15 (1960): 9.

Burns, David. *Feeling Good: The New Mood Therapy*. New York: Penguin Books, 1980.

Engstrom, I. "Family Interaction and Locus of Control in Children and Adolescents with Inflammatory Bowel Disease." *Journal of the American Academy of Child and Adolescent Psychiatry* 30:6 (1991): 913.

Freud, Sigmund. *Mourning and Melancholia* (1917). Volume 14, p. 239, in *The Standard Edition of the Complete Psychological Works of Sigmund Freud*, translated and edited by J. Strachey. London: Hogarth Press, 1968.

Gershon, E. S. et al. "Diagnoses in School-Age Children of Bipolar Affective Disorder Patients and Normal Controls." *Journal of Affective Disorders* 8 (1985): 283.

Jacobson, Edith. *Depression*. New York: International Universities Press, 1971.

Lewinsohn, Peter M. "The Behavioral Study and Treatment of Depression." In *Progress in Behavior Modification*, edited by M. Hersen, R. M. Eisler, and P. M. Miller. New York: Academic Press, 1975.

McKnew, D. H., and L. Cytryn. "Diagnoses in School-Age Children of Bipolar Affective Disorder Parents and Normal Controls." *Journal of Affective Disorders* 8 (1985): 283.

———. "Urinary Metabolites in Chronically Depressed Children." *Journal of the American Academy of Child and Adolescent Psychiatry* 18 (1979): 608.

Norris, Ronald V. *PMS: Premenstrual Syndrome*. New York: Rawson, 1983.

Puig-Antich, J. et al. "Growth Hormone Secretion in Prepubertal Children with Major Depression." *Archives of General Psychiatry* 41 (1984): 455.

Rosenthal, Norman E. *Seasons of the Mind*. New York: Bantam, 1989.

Seligman, M. E. P. et al. "Attributional Style and Depressive Symptoms Among Children." *Journal of Abnormal Psychology* 93:2 (1984): 235.

Shafii, M., and S. L. Shafii. *Clinical Guide to Depression in Children and Adolescents*. Washington, DC: American Psychiatric Press, 1992.

Spitz, Rene A. "Anaclitic Depression: An Inquiry into the Genesis of Psychiatric Conditions in Early Childhood," II. *Psychoanalytic Study of the Child* 2 (1946): 313.

Steinem, Gloria. *Revolution from Within*. Boston: Little, Brown, 1992.

Werner, Emmy G., and Ruth S. Smith. *Vulnerable but Invincible: A Study of Resilient Children*. New York: McGraw-Hill, 1982.

Chapter 4: Childhood Depression and School Failure

Bernstein, G. A., and B. D. Garfinkel. "School Phobia: The Overlap of Affective and Anxiety Disorders." *Journal of the American Academy of Child Psychiatry* 25:2 (1986): 235.

Christ, Adolph. "School Consultation." In *Child and Adolescent Psychiatry: A Comprehensive Textbook*, edited by M. Lewis. Baltimore: Williams and Wilkins, 1991.

Maag, J. W. et al. "Secondary School Professionals' Ability to Identify Depression in Adolescents." *Adolescence* 23:89 (Spring 1988): 73.

Silver, L. B. *The Misunderstood Child*. New York: McGraw-Hill, 1984.

Chapter 5: Childhood Depression and Behavior Problems

American Psychiatric Association. *Diagnostic and Statistical Manual of Mental Disorders* 3rd ed. rev. Washington, DC: American Psychiatric Association, 1987.

Earls, F. "Epidemiology and Child Psychiatry: Entering the Second Phase." *American Journal of Orthopsychiatry* 59:2 (1989): 279.

Marriage, K., S. Fine, M. Moretti, and G. Haley, "Relationship Between Depression and Conduct Disorder in Children and Adolescents." *Journal of the American Academy of Child Psychiatry* 25:5 (1986): 687.

Yates, A. "Current Perspectives on the Eating Disorders: I. History, Psychological and Biological Aspects." *Journal of the American Academy of Child Psychiatry* 28:6 (1989): 813.

Chapter 6: Childhood Depression and Substance Abuse

Fraser, Craig, and Deidre Sullivan. *Burnt: A Teenage Addict's Road to Recovery*. New York: New American Library, 1989.

Gorski, Terence T. *Understanding the Twelve Steps*. New York: Prentice-Hall, 1989.

Kandel, D. B. "Epidemiological and Psychosocial Perspectives on Adolescent Drug Use." *Journal of the American Academy of Child and Adolescent Psychiatry* 21 (1982): 328.

Morrison, M. A. "Overview: Kids and Drugs." *Psychiatric Annals* 21:2 (February 1991):72–73.

Otteson, Orlo, and John Townsend, with Tim Rumsey. *Kids and Drugs: A Parent's Guide*. New York: CFS Publishing Corp., 1983.

Polson, Beth, and Miller Newton. *Not My Kid: A Parent's Guide to Kids and Drugs*. New York: Arbor House, 1984.

Reeves, John, and James B. Austin. *How to Find Help for a Troubled Kid*. New York: Henry Holt, 1990.

Rogers, P. et al. "Adolescent Chemical Dependence: A Diagnosable Disease." *Psychiatric Annals* 21:2 (1991): 91.

Scott, Sharon. *Peer Pressure Reversal*. Amherst, MA: Human Resource Development Press, 1985.

Chapter 7: Suicide Prevention

Brent, David A. et al. "The Presence and Accessibility of Firearms in the Homes of Adolescent Suicides." *Journal of the American Medical Association* 266:21 (December 4, 1991): 2989.

Centers for Disease Control. "Attempted Suicide Among High School Students, United States, 1990." *Morbidity and Mortality Weekly Report* 40 (1991): 633.

Centers for Disease Control. "Weapon-Carrying Among High School Students, United States, 1990." *Morbidity and Mortality Weekly Report* 40 (1991): 681.

Giffin, Mary, and Carol Felsenthal. *A Cry for Help*. Garden City, NY: Doubleday, 1983.

Rutter, Michael et al., eds. *Depression in Young People*. New York: Guilford Press, 1986.

Chapter 8: All in the Family: Helping Yourself and Your Child

Canter, Lee. *Homework Without Tears: A Parents' Guide for Motivating Children to Do Homework and Succeed in School*. New York: HarperCollins, 1988.

Chapter 9: Therapy for Your Depressed Child

American Medical Association: *Drug Evaluations*. 6th ed., DE-6. Chicago: American Medical Association, 1986.

Axline, Virginia. *Play Therapy*. New York: Ballantine Books, 1947.

Beck, A. T. et al. *Cognitive Therapy for Depression*. New York: Guilford Press, 1979.

Burns, David B. *Feeling Good: The New Mood Therapy*. New York: Penguin Books, 1980.

Bush, Richard. *A Parent's Guide to Child Therapy*. New York: Delacorte Press, 1980.

Ehrenberg, Otto, and Miriam Ehrenberg. *The Psychotherapy Maze*. New York: Holt, Rinehart and Winston, 1977.

Fishman, Katherine. "Therapy for Children." *Atlantic Monthly*, June 1991, 47.

Herskowitz, Joel. *Is Your Child Depressed?* New York: Pharos Books, 1988.

Kovacs, M. "The Children's Depression Inventory (CDI)." *Psychopharmacology Bulletin* 21 (1985): 955–98.

Madanes, Chloe. *Sex, Love, and Violence.* New York: W. W. Norton, 1990.

Reaves, John, and James B. Austin. *How to Find Help for a Troubled Child.* New York: Henry Holt and Company, 1990.

Seligman, Martin. *Learned Optimism.* New York: Alfred A. Knopf, 1991.

Wilkes, T. C. R., and A. J. Rush. "Adaptations of Cognitive Therapy for Depressed Adolescents." *Journal of the American Academy of Child and Adolescent Psychiatry* 27:3 (1988): 381.

Chapter 10: Should You Hospitalize Your Depressed Child?

Abroms, G., C. Fellner, and C. Whitaker. "The Family Enters the Hospital." *American Journal of Psychiatry* 127:10 (1971): 99.

Barish, J. I., and W. A. Schonfeld. "Comprehensive Residential Treatment of Adolescents." *Current Psychiatric Therapy* 12 (1972): 9.

Easson, W. M. *The Severely Disturbed Adolescent.* New York: International Universities Press, 1969.

Feinstein, S. C., and V. Uribe. "Hospitalization of Young People: Rationale and Criteria." *Psychiatric Annals* 15:10 (1985): 602.

Fineberg, B. L., S. K. Sowards, and P. W. Kettlewell. "Adolescent Inpatient Treatment: A Literature Review." *Adolescence* 15:6 (1980): 913.

Freud, A. "The Concept of Developmental Lines." In *Normality and Pathology in Childhood* by A. Freud. New York: International Universities Press, 1965.

Hanrahan, G. "Beginning Work with Families of Hospitalized Adolescents." *Family Process* 25 (1986): 391.

Looney, J. G., M. Blotcky, D. Carson, and J. Gossett. "A Family Systems Model for Inpatient Treatment of Adolescents." *Adolescent Psychiatry* 8 (1980): 499.

Madanes, C. "The Prevention of Re-Hospitalization of Adolescents and Young Adults." *Family Process* 19 (1980): 179.

Manual of Psychiatric Peer Review. Committee on Peer Review, American Psychiatric Association. Washington, DC: 1985.

Marohn, R. C. *Juvenile Delinquents: Psychodynamic Assessment and Hospital Treatment*. New York: Brunner/Mazel, 1980.

Masterson, J. F. *Treatment of the Borderline Adolescent*. New York: Brunner/Mazel, 1985.

Miller, D. *Attack on the Self*. Northvale, NJ: Jason Aronson, 1986.

———. "The Development of Psychiatric Treatment Services for Adolescents." In *Current Issues in Adolescent Psychiatry*, edited by J. C. Schoolar. New York: Brunner/Mazel, 1973.

Rinsley, D. B. "Intensive Psychiatric Hospital Treatment of Adolescents." *Psychiatric Quarterly* 39 (1965): 405.

———. "Theory and Practice of Intensive Residential Treatment of Adolescents." *Adolescent Psychiatry* 1 (1971): 479.

———. *Treatment of the Severely Disturbed Adolescent*. New York: Jason Aronson, 1980.

Weisman, G. K. "Crisis-Oriented Residential Treatment as an Alternative to Hospitalization." *Hospital Community Psychiatry* 36:12 (1985): 1302.

Wilson, M. R., and N. Soth. "Approaching the Crisis in Adolescent Long-Term Hospitalization." *Psychiatric Annals* 15:10 (1985): 586.

Zinn, D. "Hospital Treatment of the Adolescent." In *Basic Handbook of Child Psychiatry*, edited by J. Noshpitz. New York: Basic Books, 1979.

Chapter 11: Choosing the Best Hospital

"Child and Adolescent Psychiatric Hospitalization." National Association of Private Psychiatric Hospitals, 1991.

Hersov, L., and A. Bentovim. "In-Patient and Day-Hospital Units." In *Child and Adolescent Psychiatry*, edited by M. Rutter. Boston: Blackwell, 1985.

McElroy, Evelyn, ed. *Children and Adolescents with Mental Illness: A Parent's Guide*. Kensington, MD: Woodbine House, 1988.

Petti, T. A. "Residential and Inpatient Treatment." In *Emotional Disorders in Children and Adolescents: Medical and Psychological Approaches to Treatment*, edited by B. P. Sholevar, R. Benson, and B. J. Blinder. New York: Spectrum, 1980.

Pittman, F. "Therapy Techniques of the Family Treatment Unit." In *Changing Families*, edited by J. Haley. New York: Grune and Stratton, 1971.

Stevenson, K., and M. Maholick. *Child and Adolescent Psychiatry: Guidelines for Treatment Resources, Quality Assurance, Peer Review and Reimbursement*. Washington, DC: American Academy of Child and Adolescent Psychiatry, 1987.

"When Your Child Needs Psychiatric Hospitalization." The National Association of Private Psychiatric Hospitals, 1989.

RESOURCES

Behavior Contract

The behavior contract is a contract that parents can use with childrens ages 7 to 18. Children contract with their parents to behave in an age-appropriate and responsible manner. Successful behavior is rewarded with selected privileges. For further information or a copy of the contract, write to:

Lawrence L. Kerns, M.D.
234 W. Northwest Highway, Suite 100
Barrington, IL 60010

Drugs and Alcohol

Al-Anon/Alateen
Al-Anon Family Group Headquarters Inc.
P.O. Box 862, Midtown Station
New York, NY 10018-0862
(212) 302-7240
FAX: (212) 869-3757

This organization helps anyone whose life is or has been affected by a problem drinker. Send SASE to receive more information and a list of local resources.

National Clearinghouse for Alcohol and Drug Information
11426 Rockville Pike, Suite 200
Rockville, MD 20852
(301) 468-2600
(800) 729-6686
TDD: (800) 487-4889
FAX: (301) 468-6433

A service of the Office for Substance Abuse Prevention of the federal government, NCADI offers material on current research, popular and scholarly articles, videos, public service announcements, prevention curricula, a bimonthly newsletter, and a quarterly catalog. Call or write for further information.

National Families in Action
2296 Henderson Mill Road, Suite 300
Atlanta, GA 30345
(404) 934-6364
FAX: (404) 934-7137

A national volunteer organization which sponsors the National Drug Information Center housing 500,000 documents on drug abuse; helps interested parents form Families in Action groups to organize against drug use; develops drug-education materials for use in school and public libraries; publishes a quarterly digest abstracting current articles from the medical literature.

Eating Disorders

Foundation for Education about Eating Disorders
P.O. Box 16375

Baltimore, MD 21210
(410) 467-0603

Provides pamphlets on anorexia, bulimia, and associated eating disorders, as well as a bimonthly newsletter. Call or write for pamphlets and/or a free copy of the newsletter.

National Association of Anorexia Nervosa and Associated Disorders
P.O. Box 7
Highland Park, IL 60035
(708) 831-3438

This nonprofit organization has branches in 45 states and 10 foreign countries, advocates for safe consumer products, and publishes a quarterly newsletter. To get more information on eating disorders, send SASE or call the hotline between 9 and 5 CST Monday through Friday.

Hospitalization

Joint Commission on Accreditation of Healthcare Organizations
One Renaissance Boulevard
Oakbrook Terrace, IL 60181
(708) 916-5800
FAX: (708) 916-5644

The customer service center can provide instant information on the accreditation of specific organizations.

The National Association of Private Psychiatric Hospitals
1319 F Street NW, Suite 1000
Washington, DC 20004
(202) 393-6700
FAX: (202) 783-6041

This organization represents the nation's nongovernmental free-standing hospitals that deliver psychiatric services. Accredited by the Joint Commission on Accreditation of

Healthcare Organizations, NAPPH hospitals must pass a
rigorous on-site survey conducted by NAPPH.

Learning Disabilities

Learning Disabilities Association of America
4156 Library Road
Pittsburgh, PA 15234
(412) 341-1515
FAX: (412) 344-0224

This national nonprofit organization provides general information about learning disabilities as well as referrals to
one of 700 local chapters throughout the country.

National Center for Learning Disabilities
99 Park Avenue, 6th floor
New York, NY 10016
(212) 687-7211

Formerly Foundation for Children with Learning Disabilities, this not-for-profit volunteer organization offers com-
puterized information and referral services, outreach in
the form of seminars and public policy initiatives, and an
annual publication called *Their World*. Their five-part
video series, "We Can Learn," teaches educators, parents,
and the interested public about learning disabilities and
related issues.

Children with Attention Deficit Disorder
499 Northwest 70th Avenue
Suite 308
Plantation, FL 33317
(305) 587-3700
FAX: (305) 587-4599

A national nonprofit support organization that dissemi-
nates information on attention deficit disorders and can
refer parents to one of 370 local groups.

Mental Illness, Depression

Depression and Related Affective Disorders Association
Johns Hopkins University School of Medicine
Meyer 3-181
600 North Wolfe Street
Baltimore, MD 21205
(410) 955-4647

A nonprofit organization that provides support and education for people with depression or related mental disorders. Send for pamphlet with recommended reading list.

National Alliance for the Mentally Ill
2101 Wilson Blvd., Suite 302
Arlington, VA 22201-6264
(800) 950-NAMI

This national clearinghouse can give you the name of one of more than 900 local affiliates. NAMI provides information on mental illness and services for families.

National Depressive and Manic-Depressive Association
730 North Franklin Street, Suite 501
Chicago, IL 60610
(800) 826-3632
(312) 642-0049
FAX: (312) 542-7243

A not-for-profit organization that seeks to educate the public about depression and manic-depressive disorder; develops self-help chapters around the world; publishes a quarterly newsletter.

National Foundation for Depressive Illness Inc.
P.O. Box 2257
New York, NY 10116
(800) 248-4344

Call to get a recorded message of the symptoms of depression and manic-depression and instructions on how to receive additional information. Send SASE with 98 cents postage (and a $5 donation to cover the costs of mailing, if possible) to receive a packet of information including a bibliography.

National Mental Health Association
1021 Prince Street
Alexandria, VA 22314-2971
(800) 969-6977
(703) 684-7722
FAX: (703) 684-5968

This volunteer advocacy organization concerned with all aspects of mental health and mental illness has 500 local chapters.

Premenstrual Syndrome (PMS)

PMS Access
Madison Pharmacy Associates
P.O. 9326
Madison, WI 53715
(608) 833-4PMS in Wisconsin
(800) 222-4PMS
FAX: (608) 833-7412

PMS Access provides general information and personal consultation on premenstrual syndrome; an extensive library of current literature, audio and video tapes, and slide programs; and a national bimonthly newsletter, *PMS Access*. The organization also coordinates a network of physicians, nurses, health professionals, and women with PMS, thereby linking women with support groups and health care providers.

Seasonal Affective Disorder (SAD)

Society for Light Treatment and Biological Rhythms
P.O. Box 478

Wilsonville, OR 97070
(503) 694-2404
FAX: (503) 694-2404

This organization of researchers, clinicians, and patients is dedicated to developing, evaluating, and disseminating light treatment for seasonal affective and related disorders. They offer publications and a clinician referral service. Send SASE for further information.

Suicide

American Association of Suicidology
2459 South Ash
Denver, CO 80222
(303) 692-0985
FAX: (303) 756-3299

This nonprofit organization promotes research, public awareness programs, and education for professionals and volunteers. Send SASE for more information.

Psychotherapy

American Academy of Child and Adolescent Psychiatry
3615 Wisconsin Avenue NW
Washington, DC 20016
(202) 966-7300

This professional organization for child and adolescent psychiatrists publishes a helpful series, "Facts for Families." Call or write for a catalog of materials.

American Association for Marriage and Family Therapy
1100 17th Street NW
10th floor
Washington, DC 20036-4601
(800) 374-2638

(202) 452-0109
FAX: (202) 223-2329

The professional organization for family therapists in the U.S. and Canada, AAMFT will send you a list of clinical members in your local area along with the pamphlet "A Consumer's Guide to Marriage and Family Therapy" if you call their 800 number.

American Psychological Association
750 First Street NE
Washington, DC 20002-4242
(202) 336-5500
FAX: (202) 336-5708

The world's largest association of psychologists, APA will send a list of free booklets and pamphlets on mental health issues, including depression. Send SASE.

National Association of Social Workers
750 First Street NE, Suite 700
Washington, DC 20002-4241
(202) 408-8600

NASW maintains a directory of clinical social workers throughout the country, which can be obtained by calling 1-800-638-8799.

For Further Reading

Becnel, Barbara. *Parents Who Help Their Children Overcome Drugs.* Los Angeles: Lowell House, 1989.

Burns, David. *Feeling Good: The New Mood Therapy.* New York: William Morrow, 1980.

Chiles, John. *Teenage Depression and Suicide.* New York: Chelsea House, 1986.

Clemes, Harris, and Reynold Bean. *How to Raise Children's Self-Esteem.* Los Angeles: Price Stern Sloan, 1990.

Dowling, Colette. *You Mean I Don't Have to Feel This Way?* New York: Scribner's, 1991.

Gold, Mark. *The Good News About Depression.* New York: Bantam Books, 1986.

Hafen, Brent, and Kathryn Frandsen. *Youth Suicide: Depression and Loneliness.* Evergreen, CO: Cordillera Press, 1986.

McElroy, Evelyn, ed. *Children and Adolescents with Mental Illness: A Parent's Guide.* Kensington, MD: Woodbine House, 1988.

INDEX

ABOUT THE AUTHORS

Dr. Lawrence L. Kerns graduated from Yale University. He received his medical degree from the University of Chicago's Pritzker School of Medicine and his psychiatric training at Northwestern University and the Institute of Psychiatry. The 1986 winner of a Menninger award, Dr. Kerns is assistant clinical professor of psychiatry at the University of Illinois and the Institute for Juvenile Research. In addition to his private clinical practice, he consults with several school districts and community youth agencies in northern Illinois and lectures across the country on childhood depression. Dr. Kerns and his wife have four children.

Adrienne B. Lieberman has an A.B. from Harvard University and a master's in teaching from the University of Chicago. The author of three books and numerous magazine articles, Ms. Lieberman lives with her husband and two children.